ingful. She wants a fulfilling career and has listened to feminist political organizations that say a women's primary goal should be to work full-time and make money. Amanda struggles to reconcile these perspectives with her own hopes and desires.

Can you identify with Amanda? I sure can—she was more or less me ten years ago. A lot of my peers today are learning in their thirties that they wish they'd made different decisions in their twenties. And when I speak to members of the generation just coming out of college today, I encounter women with the exact same hopes and fears that I had and who, much like me, lacked a road map for how to navigate the tumultuous terrain of adulthood.

This book is written to address the misinformation being fed to women. I'm thirty-two years old, married, and just had my first child. I know the difficulties that women face during their twenties and thirties as they make decisions that will affect the rest of their lives. I feel lucky my life has turned out as it has, but I sure wish I'd received better information when I was younger about the trade-offs women inevitably must make during their lives.

This book exposes some of the most frequent myths sold to young women and takes on taboo areas of research not discussed in the politically correct world of academia or in popular culture targeted at young women.

For too long, the feminist movement has dictated what's appropriate to talk about—and what's off-limits—when it comes to issues affecting women's lives. An ethic of silence has surrounded issues like the negative sides of casual sex, the relationship between age and infertility, and the effects of daycare and divorce on kids. This silence has real consequences for women, their families, and our society.

This book fills the knowledge gap by highlighting research in areas of critical importance to women's lives—from sex, love, and marriage to work, daycare, and divorce. It exposes how the feminist vision of what women *should* want their lives to be often runs counter to the hopes and desires of actual women.

Since this book doesn't pretend to be a comprehensive overview of research on all the topics addressed, readers interested in learning more will be pointed to other texts—works often ignored by academia and popular culture, which provide more thorough analysis. This isn't meant to endorse everything contained in those books, but I've included them because they are useful resources and offer interesting perspectives.

Women need the unvarnished truth in order to appreciate the consequences of life's choices—the decisions that shape our futures. I believe the only way to foster a generation of *truly independent* women is to present them with the best information available and then allow them to follow their hearts and minds.

A brief history of the women's movement

The first women's rights convention in the United States was held in Seneca Falls, New York, on July 19 and 20, 1848. The women who gathered there—including Elizabeth Cady Stanton and Lucretia Mott—issued a Declaration of Sentiments, which echoed the Declaration of Independence, listing grievances that women suffered in the United States and calling for equal treatment under the law:

> We hold these truths to be self-evident: that all men and women are created equal; that they are endowed by their Creator with certain inalienable rights; that among these are life, liberty, and the pursuit of happiness....
>
> The history of mankind is a history of repeated injuries and usurpations on the part of man toward woman, having in direct object the establishment of an absolute tyranny over her. To prove this, let facts be submitted to a candid world.

The **Politically Incorrect Guide**™ to

Women, Sex, and Feminism

The **Politically Incorrect Guide**™ to
Women, Sex, and Feminism

Carrie L. Lukas

Since 1947
REGNERY
PUBLISHING, INC.
An Eagle Publishing Company • Washington, DC

Cataloging-in-Publication data on file with the Library of Congress
ISBN 1-59698-003-6

Published in the United States by
Regnery Publishing, Inc.
One Massachusetts Avenue, NW
Washington, DC 20001
www.regnery.com

Distributed to the trade by
National Book Network
Lanham, MD 20706

Manufactured in the United States of America

10 9 8 7 6 5 4 3 2 1

Books are available in quantity for promotional or premium use. Write to Director of Special Sales, Regnery Publishing, Inc., One Massachusetts Avenue NW, Washington, DC 20001, for information on discounts and terms or call (202) 216-0600.

CONTENTS

Contents

WOMEN'S UNINFORMED CHOICES

*A*ccording to a poll conducted by *Marie Claire*, one-third of women consider themselves to be feminists. But what does being a feminist mean today, some forty years after the birth of the modern feminist movement? After all, since 1963, we've had Betty Friedan, Gloria Steinem, Germaine Greer, and the National Organization for Women, the Feminist Majority, and *Ms* Magazine, capture the popular imagination, influence successive generations of women, and define what it means to be a feminist. The politically correct answer from the leaders of the feminist movement would be that they believe in women's equality. It's a good answer; just about everyone believes that women should be treated fairly and equitably. The problem is that since 1963, real feminism, organized feminism, has evolved into something altogether different.

The modern feminist movement isn't about women's equality. It's about an agenda designed to benefit a special interest group: women who will follow the professional feminist's idea of what a woman *should* want. To further this agenda, the modern feminist movement takes to the airways, Internet, and the print media, and walks the halls of Congress, the federal government, and state capitols to expand government, subsidize politically correct choices for women, and change our culture so that men and women become interchangeable. They also work hand-in-hand with liberal colleges to advance these goals.

The feminist influence on our government, media, and educational system means that many young women are getting a lot of bad information. And bad information leads to bad decisions that are especially harmful when they are made by young women, just starting off on their own.

Consider the many important decisions that a young woman—let's call her Amanda—will make during the following ten years of her life. Amanda worked hard in high school to get into a good college. She has a nice group of friends and enjoys average college-girl activities—she reads magazines like *Cosmopolitan* and *Glamour*, indulges in *Desperate Housewives* and re-runs of *Sex in the City*, but always manages to complete her studies. Soon, she'll have a degree from a respected university and be poised to begin the next stage of life.

She'll get a job and start down a career path. She'll meet potential mates and may consider getting married. She'll make important health decisions: She may consider engaging in casual sex and may face the decision of whether to have an abortion. She'll think about having children. If she decides to begin building a family, she'll face choices about her role as a parent and how to balance family with career aspirations. She may also consider divorce.

Does Amanda have the information she needs to make decisions that will improve her chances for long-term health and happiness?

Unfortunately, the answer is no. Most likely, she's been given a lot of bad information, much of it in the name of political correctness.

Amanda grew up in a culture that makes it difficult for her to describe right from wrong—she fears being judgmental. Even as she hopes for marriage, she sees divorce as the natural end for marriages that aren't entirely happy. She's been saturated by popular culture that glorifies promiscuity, and reads feminist literature telling her that it's old fashioned to associate sex with marriage and love. She's sometimes confused about the role sex should play in her own life, whether she should view it as a casual activity meant simply for pleasure, or as something more mean-

He has never permitted her to exercise her inalienable right to the elective franchise....

He has endeavored, in every way that he could, to destroy her confidence in her own powers, to lessen her self-respect, and to make her willing to lead a dependent and abject life.

Now, in view of this entire disfranchisement of one-half the people of this country, their social and religious degradation—in view of the unjust laws above mentioned, and because women do feel themselves aggrieved, oppressed, and fraudulently deprived of their most sacred rights, we insist that they have immediate admission to all the rights and privileges which belong to them as citizens of the United States.

These pioneers for women's equality are often referred to as "first-wave" feminists. The women's rights movement of the nineteenth and early twentieth century focused primarily on gaining the right to vote for women. This goal was achieved in 1919 with the passage of the 19th Amendment.

The "second-wave" of feminism occurred during the 1960s and 1970s when women began pushing for legal and social changes that would allow them to participate more fully in society and the economy. Many herald the start of feminism's second-wave with the release of the book *The Feminist Mystique* by Betty Friedan. This book described the dissatisfaction that many housewives felt with their situation and encouraged women to consider work outside the home. This message resonated with many women, and many of them joined to press for political and social changes.

The "second-wave" feminists demanded guarantees of women's equal treatment under the law and an end to gender-based discrimination. They sought also to change societal expectations for women. Some of these changes included simply encouraging women to take jobs and roles that had traditionally been reserved for men. However, some feminists took the desire for more options a step further and became overtly hostile to the traditional roles that women had played. They questioned—and at times fought to undermine—the concept of the nuclear family. They saw men not as equal partners, but as enemies who oppress women. They encouraged women to forgo traditional relationships and embrace sexual "liberation." During this period—and in part due to the feminist movement's influence—Americans' attitudes towards sex shifted dramatically, including more openness to premarital sex, and family structures began to shift, with the divorce and out-of-wedlock births soaring.

The modern feminist movement

Today, the feminist movement—which encompasses what is sometimes referred to as feminism's "third-wave"—has grown into a large, organized, politically powerful entity that wields tremendous influence over public policy, on college campuses, and in popular culture. While the second-wave of feminism primarily addressed the concerns of white, straight, relatively well-off women, the modern feminist movement focuses a great deal on the concerns of lesbians, minority women, and those living in poverty.

In many ways, the feminist movement of today is a victim of its own successes. *Webster's Dictionary* defines feminism as "the doctrine advocating social, political, and all other rights of women equal to those of men" and "an organized movement for the attainment of such rights for women."[1] But this battle has been won: Overwhelmingly, Americans expect and support the idea that women and men are equal and deserve equal opportunity and treatment under the law.

Modern feminism has strayed far from this original mission. It is now associated with radical liberal politics, including support for an ever larger federal government, a European-style welfare state, and a general hostility to traditional families. For this reason, a minority of American women today associate themselves with the label "feminist."

Chapter One

THE DIFFERENCE
BETWEEN BOYS AND GIRLS

*A*re there innate differences between the sexes? The politically correct answer is "no." Although feminist educators acknowledge that it's impossible to ignore differences in the male and female anatomies, many insist—often stridently—that the behavioral characteristics we commonly associate with female and male are social constructs.

Their general opposition, for some blind hostility, to any discussion of innate gender differences is an important backdrop to understanding some of the challenges that women face today—and how feminists advance a vision and agenda that's contrary to many women's desires and interests.

The controversy about gender

In January 2005, then Harvard University president Lawrence Summers spoke at an academic conference dedicated to exploring the question of why women are under-represented in the fields of science and math at top universities. Larry Summers, who served as secretary of the treasury under President Clinton, is hardly a conservative ideologue. But at this conference, Summers made the mistake of delving into the controversial subject of gender differences.

Summers suggested some causes for the dearth of women in the upper echelons of science and math. He mentioned the possibility of discrimi-

Guess what?

- Former Harvard University president Lawrence Summers was censured by the Harvard faculty for speculating about the innate differences between men and women.

- Research suggests that men's and women's brains are built differently.

- The weight of scientific research—and simple observation—leads to the politically incorrect conclusion that gender is not a social construct.

1

What a Feminist Icon Said:

"The trouble with The Women's Revolution is that we have not gone far enough because we indulge our fathers, husbands, brothers, sons. Also we feel sorry for them because they are led around by their d—s and their brains go soft. We accept the burden of being rational cause we know they're testosterone-driven."

—Erica Jong

http://www.ericajong.com/interviewwitherica.htm

nation and women's desires for more flexible schedules than lab-intensive professions allow. He also speculated that innate differences between the genders could contribute to women's under-representation at the top of these fields.

This set off a firestorm. Nancy Hopkins, a Massachusetts Institute of Technology biology professor in attendance at the conference, described nearly fainting after hearing Summers. Recovering, she quickly ran to the media to voice her complaints. The media were listening. In front page news stories and countless hours of television punditry, Summers's heresy was dutifully reported and discussed. Finally, Harvard's faculty met and censured Summers with a vote of "no confidence."

The besieged university president must have realized that endless apologies weren't going to satisfy Harvard's gender warriors. So he offered $50 million for initiatives to encourage "diversity"—meaning "more women," not more points of view—within the faculty.

What did Summers say that was so wrong? He didn't suggest that a woman couldn't achieve as much as a man in the fields of science and math. He merely suggested that biological differences *may* contribute to a statistical outcome for women as a group.

Summers learned his lesson and undoubtedly won't make the mistake again of engaging in such open academic inquiry. Other academics surely learned a similar lesson. What young professor, hoping for tenure, is going to dare question the tenants of feminism in her research? What PhD student, looking forward to defending her dissertation, is eagerly going to pursue evidence that men *do* exhibit on average a greater aptitude for science? It may be commonly accepted that women have stronger innate verbal abilities, but identifying similar strengths in men is academic treason.

The Larry Summers controversy is just one episode in a larger and highly contentious debate about gender differences; differences that most people with common sense see in everyday life and consider natural.

Nature or nurture?

Many feminists recoil at the suggestion that there could be innate differences between men and women and imagine a gender-free world. In his book, *Taking Sex Differences Seriously*, Dr. Steven Rhoads reveals how these attitudes aren't just common within the fringe of the feminist movement: It is dogma that dominates much of the feminist movements' agenda.

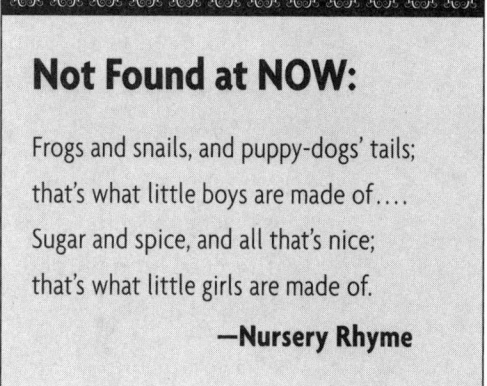

Not Found at NOW:

Frogs and snails, and puppy-dogs' tails; that's what little boys are made of.... Sugar and spice, and all that's nice; that's what little girls are made of.

—Nursery Rhyme

For example, one academic theorist, Susan Okin, envisions a future in which "one's sex would have no more relevance than one's eye color or the length of one's toes," and men and women would participate in "more or less equal numbers in every sphere of life." Another feminist theorist wants women and men to be seen as "socially interchangeable."[1]

These feminists see achieving a genderless society as a realistic goal because they believe the traits we label as "masculine" and "feminine" are nothing more than social constructs thrust upon us as children. Little girls are welcomed into the world with pink blankets, cuddly dolls, and gussied-up Barbies; they're encouraged to play house with friends and read fairytale stories. Little boys are greeted with blue blankets, trucks, and building blocks; they're encouraged to run around and compete with their playmates. In doing so, children are indoctrinated to behave in ways associated with their "assigned" gender.

Since these cultural forces are artificial, they can be changed. By raising awareness among parents and encouraging them to fight these habits—and by enacting public policies that dictate what occurs in schools—it might be possible to change social norms. Therefore, if gender really is just a social construct, the feminist dream of an androgynous society could become reality.

Much to the chagrin of the feminist movement, the facts don't support their theory. Researchers continue to turn up evidence that the behavioral differences we observe in men and women are rooted in biological sex differences. One piece of evidence that is difficult to refute is the universal aspects of the roles assumed by males and females. Rhoads highlights the work of one theorist who "takes no pleasure" in recognizing some aspects of the gender breakdown—such as men's greater aggression and domination of "the public sphere"—but acknowledges how these gender differences appear throughout history and across cultures.[2]

Sometimes, this evidence can even change minds. One researcher entered the field with the intention of debunking the notion that differences in behavior and cognition are biologically based. After reviewing the enormous amount of research on the topic, she changed her mind. "There are real, and in some cases sizeable, sex differences with respect to some cognitive abilities," she said. "Socialization practices are undoubtedly important, there is also good evidence that biological sex differences play a role."[3]

Rhoads describes a similar evolution of thought occurring when those committed to a gender neutral world have children. One feminist was attempting to bring her young son up in a sensitive, non-violent, gender-neutral

A Book You're Not Supposed to Read

Taking Sex Differences Seriously, Steven E. Rhoads; San Francisco, Encounter Books, 2004.

manner, but her son developed an insatiable obsession with guns. With no toy guns in the house, he used other toys and even food to construct make-shift guns. Another feminist struggled with a daughter who refused to wear anything but dresses and stockings.[4]

Root causes of the differences between men and women

Research suggests that men's and women's brains are built differently, which may be a root cause of some of the different characteristics that we associate with men and women.[5] Men's left and right brain hemispheres are connected by fewer neurons than are women's and men's brains tend to be more "compartmentalized" while women's are "networked." Researchers hypothesize that this may be the reason why women are better at verbal disciplines, while men excel at spatial tasks.

Hormonal differences also have been shown to drive behavioral characteristics. Researchers studied girls who, while in the womb, were exposed to high levels of testosterone—a hormone found in both girls and boys, but in much higher levels in males. These girls exhibited many of the behaviors commonly associated with boys, such as greater aggression, engaging in more "rough-and-tumble" play, and preferring mechanical toys, such as trucks and building materials, over dolls and crafts—the typical choice of girls.[6]

Other studies of adult women with higher testosterone levels found that these women exhibited more stereotypically masculine characteristics such as being more assertive and career oriented, having a higher self-regard, greater interest in casual sex, and superior spatial skills.[7]

The fact that men and women are hard-wired differently would explain why masculine and feminine characteristics appear universally throughout history and around the globe. But this concept doesn't fit in with feminist dogma, which is why it remains so controversial.

Why sex differences matter

Feminists have a vision: To see men and women represented equally in all disciplines and in all walks of life. They lament that women still assume disproportionate responsibility for housework and childcare, have lower levels of achievement in business and politics, and gravitate away from disciplines like math and science.

What's the cause of women's lack of progress in these areas?

According to the feminists, society, and the discriminatory, sexist attitudes that still lurk among us are to blame.

If you accept these assumptions, then something can—and indeed should—be done. So long as society is at fault, then the feminist vision can theoretically become reality by changing public education, creating government-subsidized daycare, encouraging more mothers to leave their children for the workforce, and many other measures that change society.

If, however, men and women's differences are not social constructs—if they are instead the product of innate, biological differences—then no amount of government intervention will create the feminist utopia. Indeed, if gender differences are natural, then the feminist idea of progress isn't progress at all, and their agenda makes men and women worse off by driving them away from their true preferences in pursuit of a feminist fantasy.

The weight of scientific research—and simple observation—leads to the politically incorrect conclusion that gender is not a social construct. Undoubtedly, socialization plays a role in shaping our behavior; but sex differences strongly influence who we are as humans. Among other things, this means that women and men will have dissimilar preferences and reactions in many situations—an important consideration when we examine how the feminist vision for our country often stands in opposition to women's instincts and expressed interests.

Chapter Two

RETURN TO ROMANCE

Traditional dating and courtship have all but disappeared for teenagers and twenty-somethings. For decades, feminists have disparaged traditional gender roles in romantic relationships as sexist and stifling for women. Men who open doors and offer to pay aren't gentlemen—they're misogynists objectifying women and perpetuating "patriarchy." Feminists celebrate the sexual revolution and encourage women to break away from traditional dating practices and approach relationships more like men.

What has this meant for young women? Ironically, many young women have experienced a loss of power in the post-sexual revolution dating environment.

Overwhelmingly, young women still see marriage as an important goal, and most college women hope to meet their future husbands before they graduate. But it's not the 1950s and women need to be aware of some of the pitfalls of the new romantic terrain and recognize the important roles that more traditional dating and courtship play in building healthy relationships.

Guess what?

- Overwhelmingly, young women still see marriage as an important goal.

- Research shows that women still tend to prefer men who are breadwinners, who they can consider intellectually superior, and who can physically protect them.

- Research also shows that men prefer fertile, loyal women.

Feminists' hostility to chivalry

Women's studies textbooks often include a passage on fairytales. A little girl, they say, is told from infancy that her highest aspiration should be to earn the love of a prince who will save her, protect her, and enable her to live happily ever after. Cinderella, an obedient, quiet, beautiful young girl, beaten down by loud, ugly step sisters, is rewarded for her good behavior by winning the hand of a handsome prince. Sleeping Beauty and Snow White lie unconscious until they're kissed by their princes.

To many feminists, these are the quintessential messages given to girls about their role in society. Feminists see the traditional roles assumed by men and women during courtship as sexist and demeaning to women. Men, they say, had too much power in traditional courtship. Men were expected to take the lead—by pursuing a woman, initiating contact, paying the costs of activities, and giving gifts as tokens of affection—while women were left to react to their advances. It was taboo for a woman to call a man, initiate contact, or pay for her own share of any expenses incurred during a date.

The unevenness of the male-female economic relationship in traditional courtship was particularly abhorrent to many feminists. The implication of allowing men to assume the financial burden associated with courtship was that men were essentially "buying" time with the woman or that the woman was for sale. Courtship was seen as a time for men to demonstrate their ability to support a future mate financially, suggesting that women were expected to depend on their future husbands economically and incapable of providing for themselves.

Gestures once expected from gentlemen—such as opening doors or giving up seats to women—were no longer viewed as chivalrous, but evidence that men assumed women were somehow weak and less capable. According to radical feminists' logic, a man who offers to carry a woman's heavy bags implies she needs a man's assistance to get along.

Will You Be My Vagina?

*T*he phenomenon of *The Vagina Monologues* and advent of "V-Day" on college campuses perfectly encapsulates the feminists' hostility to romance.

The Vagina Monologues is a play consisting of a series of vignettes that describe the experiences of numerous women's vaginas: from heterosexual and lesbian sex to child birth, with a particular focus on violence and rape. *The Monologues* first was performed in 1998, and today appears on college campuses throughout the country during the week of February 14—Valentine's Day.

Instead of celebrating romantic love with flowers and candy, students are encouraged to celebrate "V-Day" by watching a fairly raunchy play that, among other things, encourages the audience to join in with the actress in yelling the word "c——."

Attending *The Vagina Monologues* isn't the only way to celebrate V-Day. Some campus groups have taken to handing out vagina shaped lollipops or other goodies; others have had people dress up as giant vaginas and walk around campus. V-Day is a strange mix of the runaway sexualization of campus and the de-romanticizing of sex by reducing it to its most basic biology.

In addition to "celebrating" their vaginas and sexuality, V-Day also is a time for women to raise awareness about violence against women. As the V-Day website states, the mission is simple: "It demands that the violence must end. It proclaims Valentine's Day as V-Day until the violence stops."

Certainly raising money and awareness to fight violence against women is a worthy goal. But why the assault on Valentine's Day? The clear implication is that violence and male/female relations are somehow naturally linked and that traditional romance is detrimental to women.

Women need to reclaim Valentine's Day as a time to celebrate the important, positive role that love and romance play in women's lives.

As the traditions governing men's behavior were called into question and radically altered, expectations for women also changed. Women were encouraged to take a more active role in the courtship process. Old conventions, like those dictating that a woman not call a man or initiate a date, were thrown out. The expectation that women would serve as sexual gatekeepers—preventing their suitors from "going too far"—was also challenged: Feminists insisted that women have just as strong sex drives as men and shouldn't deny their impulses. They rebelled against the system that had imbued a woman's virginity with "virtue" and demonized sexually active women.

The important role of courtship

These traditions and roles weren't simply a means of objectifying women or installing men in positions of power. Courtship had evolved as a way for individuals to get to know each other. Men and women would typically date several different people, assessing their compatibility as long-term marriage partners, before any significant relationship began. As a relationship became more serious, courtship was a way of testing and demonstrating commitment.

Mary Elizabeth Podles, a writer on the subject of courtship, described its important role this way:

> In serious courtship, a man conveys to a woman that if she is worth all this trouble to court, she must be worth more than any mate in the world and shall henceforth be The One Woman. On her part, the woman promises that if she was this hard for him to get, surely she will, as his wife, be impossible for others to get. The courtship dance is the unspoken pledge of future fidelity—the best basis for a happy marriage.[1]

The different roles that men and women assumed in these dating rituals clearly were gender specific and could be seen as "sexist." But this negative perspective ignores the reality that men and women *do* assume different roles in romantic relationships; that they have different needs and vulnerabilities; and, that they tend to prefer members

A Book You're Not Supposed to Read

A Return to Modesty: Rediscovering the Lost Virtue, by Wendy Shalit; New York, Free Press, 2000.

of the opposite sex who possess the characteristics usually associated with that gender.

Research shows that women still tend to prefer men who are breadwinners, who they can consider intellectually superior, and who can physically protect them.[2] Men prefer fertile, loyal women, so they can be assured of their paternity and that their children will receive the care necessary to reach maturity. It's no accident or conspiracy that traditional courtship rituals allowed participants to showcase these prized qualities.

But if traditional courtship has disappeared, what traditions have taken its place? Clearly men and women are continuing to form relationships and marry, so a new form of "courtship" must have developed.

An analysis of the modern romantic landscape reveals that while there are new ways of courting, many have significant pitfalls, which traditional courtship avoided. Chief among these is failing to allow room for men and women to identify promising partners and encouraging the creation of stable, lasting relationships.

The brave new world of romance

Today, dates where a man actually asks a woman out have become rare. One study of college women found that just half of college seniors had been asked on six or more dates since college, and one-third had been asked on fewer than two dates.[3]

What has replaced traditional courtship? In a report published by the Independent Women's Forum, researchers Norval Glenn, professor of sociology at the University of Texas, and Elizabeth Marquardt, an affiliate scholar at the Institute for American Values, surveyed 1,000 college women from across the country and identified several different types of relationships that young men and women commonly enter into.

The first type of interaction they identified is what's known as "hooking up." While the exact definition of hooking up varies, basically it alludes to sexual interaction that could be anything from kissing to intercourse without commitment. Hooking up typically takes place between people who don't know each other very well and is usually fueled by alcohol. A hook up could occur as a one-time interaction or could include a series of events; in either case, it's understood that there's no obligation to continue the relationship. About 40 percent of those surveyed had "hooked up" at least once and one in ten had hooked up more than six times.

On the other end of the spectrum is what the researchers refer to as a "joined at the hip" relationship. In this serious relationship, the couple is typical sexually active, spends most of their time together, including sleeping in each others rooms, and is exclusive romantically.

Another common form of relationship identified by the researchers is "hanging out," which is sometimes referred to as "dating." A man and woman who are friends may arrange to interact, often in groups, sometimes alone, but their interest in each other is not explicitly acknowledged. Ultimately, these relationships could become more overtly romantic or physical, evolving into "hooked up" or a "joined at the hip" status.

Interviews with college women revealed a notable lack of rules or concrete understanding about the expectations within these relationships. Women who hooked up were often left wondering if the guy was going to take another step and if the relationship could evolve into something more meaningful.

None of these structures fills the role of traditional courtship in allowing women (and men) to explore the potential for meaningful relationships with prospective partners in an effort to identify the most promising, even though finding a spouse is still a goal of most women.

In some ways, men and women are more equal in these modern relationships—women can initiate hook ups and are partners in arranging "hanging out" activities. Men no longer have to take the initiative, while women have adopted more of the traditional male ethic of viewing sex as desirable outside of marriage or a committed relationship. What's less clear is what women have gained from these new, more "equal" relationships.

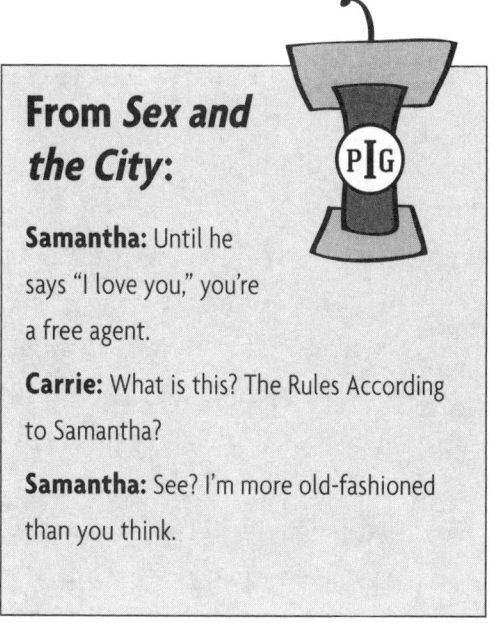

From *Sex and the City*:

Samantha: Until he says "I love you," you're a free agent.

Carrie: What is this? The Rules According to Samantha?

Samantha: See? I'm more old-fashioned than you think.

Women's loss of power

Even though it's more acceptable for women to act like men in a post-sexual revolution world, women have also ceded a great deal of power to men.

In traditional dating rituals, it's the man who must put himself on the line, risking rejection by asking a woman out. But after hooking up, the woman is often left wondering about the guy's intentions—whether he's ever going to call or see her again—and she's relatively powerless.[4] Glenn and Marquardt noted how often women were left waiting for the men to dictate the terms of their relationships. Is it just a hook up? Are we just hanging out, or dating exclusively? The women were reluctant to push the men to clarify the nature of the relationships and sometimes described "finding out" that her partner considered her his "girlfriend" from a third party source.

Much of this loss of power stems from the increased availability of sex for men. Traditionally, women's ability and willingness to withhold sexual gratification served as a way to discipline men's behavior. If a man wanted to have sex with a woman, he had to woo her, demonstrate his sincere interest and attachment to her, invest in their relationship, and promise to assume the potential consequences of sexual intimacy.

Today, often little or nothing is expected from men by the women who sleep with them. Those who "hook up" don't expect a phone call, while even those "joined at the hip" don't necessarily expect their relationships to last (most likely it will end in a heart-wrenching breakup). Men can enjoy the many benefits of marriage—not just sexually, but also the companionship and improved lifestyle that comes with having a woman who

The Morning After: A Cost–Benefit Analysis

*N*ow, I'm not out to question your right to have sex if you get horny or lonely. Second-wave feminists fought for that right, and you were most likely born with it. It's no longer about ensuring your right to pursue pleasure. It's yours, sista, so use it as you see fit. But use it wisely. Think about how you wield that power and what the costs are of sleeping with guys you might not be that into. Trust me, he's getting something out of the bargain, but what are you getting?

—Ian Kerner, Ph.D, *Be Honest—You're Not That Into Him Either*

may be happy to cook and clean for them—but without offering any commitment or support in return. Men in these relationships are still free to survey their options in case a better (prettier, smarter, younger, etc.) candidate comes along.

As a result, many young women find themselves in relationships headed nowhere with men who are unwilling to make a commitment. In *Sex in the City*, the main characters were constantly making excuses for men who didn't follow through in relationships. One of Carrie's (played by Sarah Jessica Parker) boyfriends finally explained that when guys act that way, it's simply because "he's just not that into you." This concept was so revolutionary that two *Sex and the City* writers wrote a book on the subject that quickly became a bestseller.

He's Just Not That Into You urges women to expect more from men and not make excuses for those who don't call, are married, cheat, treat them poorly, or refuse to commit. Implicit in this common sense advice is that men often hold more cards than do women in the modern dating game. Women are more likely to want to marry and, due to fertility concerns, feel more pressure and desire to marry earlier than men. As a result, it's women who often feel helpless while men dictate the nature of their relationships.

This blockbuster book was quickly followed with a slightly different book and take on the subject. In *Be Honest—You're Not That Into Him Either: Raise Your Standards and Reach for the Love You Deserve*, author and sex counselor Dr. Ian Kerner urges young women to be aware of how they are slipping into dysfunctional relationships with men that they never liked in the first place. This book is far from a call for women to embrace traditional sexual morals—Kerner celebrates the availability of vibrators and some women's willingness and ability to have sex for sex's sake. But it does highlight the practical problems that women face in the new dating arena.

Kerner hesitates to suggest that women should withhold sex from men as a way of avoiding dysfunctional relationships. He probably recognizes that this is an incredibly politically incorrect conclusion. Yet he can't entirely avoid it:

> The potential downside to a scenario where women are as aggressive as men, and where casual sex is an accepted norm, is that the biggest beneficiary of this female empowerment is the male. This is not to say that women should play by certain "rules" or withhold sex. That does not work, and it's silly gamesmanship. Or is it?

In fact, women seem hungry for "rules" on how to "win" the dating game. In 1996, when the book entitled *The Rules: Time-Tested Secrets for Capturing the Heart of Mr. Right* was released, it was a smash hit. *The Rules* purported to give women a roadmap to reclaiming the upper hand in relationships and ultimately to winning a husband. Feminists—and many others—recoiled at this old fashion guide, which offered antiquated advice like "never call a man first" and "don't accept a Saturday date after Wednesday," arguably reducing the process of falling in love to a manipulative recipe of dos and don'ts. While these specific mandates may seem jarring and out of place today, they essentially encourage women to reclaim their power by restricting men's access to them.

But even women who attempt to follow "The Rules" and change the modern dating dynamic by personally adopting more conventional standards for relationships—such as reserving sex for marriage or delaying sex until a serious monogamous relationship—are affected by the realities of the feminist dating era. A woman who wishes to maintain her virginity until marriage must compete with women willing to have sex before marriage and often without commitment. Her power to control a man and encourage him to offer commitment and marriage, in exchange for greater intimacy, is limited by the ready availability of sex elsewhere.

Rebuilding courtship

Glenn and Marquardt offer a few prescriptions for improving the quality of the social environment that young adults face. Among their recommendations are for parents to monitor the activities of their children with the goal of encouraging healthier relationships between young men and women. They highlight, for example, how men's roles in relationships have become increasingly passive and that men should be encouraged to take greater initiative with women.

Similarly Wendy Shalit, who wrote *A Return to Modesty* shortly after graduating college, emphasizes how young men and women long for greater interference and guidance from their parents. Popular culture often derides parents who attempt to limit their children's activities, particularly their daughters, calling such parents "repressive." But boundaries are important in helping young women and men avoid heartbreak and create the foundation for lasting happiness.

This doesn't mean that we need to turn the clock back to an era where women waited by the phone and never initiated a first kiss. But it's important for young women (and men) to be aware of the pitfalls of modern dating and to consider how to create a culture more conducive to healthy, lasting relationships.

Talking Points: Finding Mr. Right

- Don't Meet Him Halfway or Go Dutch on a Date
- Don't Call Him and Rarely Return His Calls
- Don't Accept a Saturday Night Date after Wednesday
- Always End the Date First
- Don't Open Up Too Fast
- No More Than Casual Kissing on the First Date
- Don't Rush Into Sex

The Rules: Time-Tested Secrets for Capturing the Heart of Mr. Right, Ellen Fein and Sherrie Schneider; New York, Free Press, 1996.

Top Ten Things Young Women Need to Know (That Feminists Won't Tell Them!)

10. Flowers, candy, and opened doors aren't weapons of oppression. Chivalrous gestures show a guy actually respects you and may be interested in a relationship.

9. You're most fertile in your twenties. During your thirties, fertility declines and many women have trouble getting pregnant after age 35. Plan ahead!

8. Discrimination isn't why women make less money than men. Women make different choices and have different priorities which results in them earning less.

7. Condoms are not a get-out-of-STD-free device—condoms do little or nothing to prevent the spread of several serious STDs.

6. Kids raised by their parents tend have fewer emotional and behavioral problems than kids who spend long hours in daycare.

5. Not everyone is doing it. Fewer of your peers than you think are engaging in casual sex—and those who are often regret it.

4. There's no shamed in aspiring to marry—married people tend to be happier, healthier, and better off financially.

3. Divorce doesn't erase a marriage—it often creates a new set of problems for you and your children.

2. You should make goals in your personal life just like you do in your career.

1. Being a woman doesn't make you a victim. You have choices to make, and to live with. That's what being liberated and independent is all about.

Chapter Three

SEX: LOVE'S GOT
SOMETHING TO DO WITH IT

A young woman reading *Cosmopolitan* or watching popular television could easily assume that she's falling down on the job of being a liberated woman unless she's engaging in casual sex. Feminists long have lamented how society has idealized women's virtue and encouraged them to be sexual gate keepers. Feminists cheered the sexual revolution that made casual sex more acceptable.

In reality, women lost the sexual revolution. Women are still more vulnerable than men, and while many women have embraced a casual sexual ethic, they often express regret after engaging in casual sex and lament their inability to separate sex from love. There's good reason for why women invest emotion in sex and young women should recognize the benefits of embracing an ethic that reserves sex for committed, monogamous relationships.

Popular culture's love affair with sex

In the world of women's magazines, sex is a recreational activity. Just as a magazine on fishing or cooking offers readers helpful tips for how to get the most enjoyment out of these hobbies, so it is with many women's magazines and sex. Nearly every magazine's cover features a sex-sational

Guess what?

- Women lost the sexual revolution.

- Women are still more vulnerable than men and lament their inability to separate sex from love.

- Many women regret casual sex, not just immediately, but also years later when they've married or finally found the love of their lives.

headline, exemplified by such classic *Cosmo* how-to manuals as "Cosmo's Below-the-Belt Guide" (March 2005), "Sex Treats for Him" (April 2005), and "Super Sensual Sex Touch Him Tricks" (May 2005), but not to be outdone by other hard-hitting pieces such as "His Butt: What Your Guy's Bum Shape Reveals about His Personality" (*Cosmopolitan*, February 2005).

These aren't tips for how to treat your husband or boyfriend; they're for any man with whom you happen decide to go to bed. Take the August 2005 issue of *Marie Claire.* It includes one story entitled "Could Your Guy Pick the Perfect Sex Toy for You?" in which two couples selected a pot-pourri of sex toys with which to surprise each other and reported back on their reactions. One couple—they've been dating for just five months—reported: "The blindfold and the handcuffs were great. And I loved the body paint and the idea of actually painting *on* the nude for a change! My surprise favorite was the paddle. . . . the exchange really confirmed how compatible we are, sexually, and otherwise."

A few pages later young female readers are presented with "13 Sex Lies You Need to Know!" The important myths debunked in this article include "ex sex is always a bad idea," "sleeping with a coworker in a no-no," and "you have to be in the mood every time you have sex." Another article contains amusing quotes from "ordinary" women answering the question, "What Are You Really Thinking about during Sex?" The women respond with such romantic sentiments as "So glad you remember my name—now will you please stop saying it?" "I can't believe that hot guy from last night didn't call. I hope he calls later!" and "Yup, he's a virgin."

Not only do such articles, regularly featured in magazines catering to young women, depict sex as an amusing, meaningless hobby, they also perpetuate the belief that everyone is having sex and lots of it. A woman who isn't "taking charge of her sexuality" and engaging numerous lovers is missing out.

This theme is echoed in "must see" television shows like *Friends*, which repeats endlessly on cable networks in the evenings. Characters who hit a "sexual dry spell" of more than a few months are mocked or receive sympathy for their unusual predicament. Casual sex is also the foundation of many reality television shows targeted to teens, such as *The Real World*. This series is contrived with the explicit purpose of putting unattached, attractive, college age kids in an intimate living situation, making alcohol readily available, in order to encourage a barrage of sexual situations. The characters that entangle themselves in the most sexual adventures are rewarded with the most airtime and often end up as pseudo-celebrities. And, of course, in the popular HBO show *Sex and the City*, the main characters engage countless lovers, often with no expectation of or desire for commitment.

These shows visibly influence young women. *Sex in the City* created a rash of aspiring young sex journalists on campuses throughout the country. Natalie Krinsky, author of *Chloe Does Yale*, launched her writing career with a sex column for the *Yale Daily News*, featuring headlines like "Spit or swallow: It's all about the sauce." Meghan Bainum, sex columnist for *The University Daily Kansan,* ended up posing in *Playboy*. Both credited *Sex in the City* as their inspiration.[1] To these young women—and most sex columnists in college newspapers are women—no topic is out of bounds. The clear, underlying message of their columns is that sex, and lots of it, is an expected part of being a college student.

Of course, this expectation doesn't end in college. Increasingly our pop culture seems to celebrate—even while still sneering at—infamously promiscuous young women. Monica Lewinsky, the intern who nearly brought down a president with her thong-snapping seduction, forever changed the image of the D.C. junior staffer from aspiring policy wonk to sexual temptress. Monica may have become the butt of a national joke, but she also reaped many rewards from her notoriety. During her twenties, this otherwise unexceptional rich girl opened her own handbag line and hosted, however temporarily, a really bad reality television show.

Now other young women appear willing to follow in her footsteps. Jessica Cutler—at the time a staffer on Capitol Hill—began Internet blogging about her various sexual adventures with a half dozen men. When the blog was linked to some prominent Washington websites, Jessica scored instant notoriety. She was quickly fired from her job, but ultimately cashed in, at least financially. Jessica posed in *Playboy* and was reportedly advanced in excess of $100,000 to write a book based on her experience, *The Washingtonienne: A Novel.*[2]

When interviewed, Jessica comes off as a sympathetic character who is trying to make the best of a bad situation. But it's disturbing that many girls see a pot of gold at the end of promiscuity's rainbow if they're willing to set shame aside.

Women's studies textbooks or *Cosmopolitan*?

If few are surprised that popular culture sends the message that sexual promiscuity is an adventurous and fulfilling part of life, some may be taken aback that this message is echoed in academia. Christina Stolba, writing for the Independent Women's Forum, reviewed the syllabi for introductory women's studies courses published by thirty colleges and found that just a few textbooks were used, and used frequently, in these classes.[3] I read these (and others that popped up on Amazon) and was often stunned by the questionable information presented as truth to America's students.

In these textbooks, sexual exploration is a key element of women's liberation. The impulse to confine sex within marriage or a committed relationship comes from that evil, amorphous institution dubbed "patriarchy." It's patriarchy that created a system under which women had to serve as sexual gatekeepers and linked virginity with virtue. Embracing this creed of sexual modesty is likened to embracing oppression.

Why is that girl yelling at her boyfriend? Oh, she just came from her women's studies class.

"In patriarchy, women in our sexual roles are to function ideally not as self-affirming, self-fulfilling human beings but rather as beautiful dolls to be looked at, touched, felt, experienced for arousal . . . to be enjoyed, consumed, and ultimately used up and traded in for a different model thing. . . . Our sexual role in patriarchy is to be acted upon, not to act ourselves, except insofar as this serves the users' interest or needs."

> **—Shelia Ruth,** *Issues in Feminism: An Introduction to Women's Studies*

"Female sexuality . . . is seen as something to be contained and controlled, as we see in the traditional dichotomy of labeling women either as virgins or as whores. Such labels depict female sexuality as evil and dangerous if not constrained and imply that "good girls" repress their sexual feelings."

> **—Margaret L. Anderson,** *Thinking About Women: Sociological Perspectives on Sex and Gender*

"The prevailing script for sexual morality is the double standard which restricts women's sexual behavior more than men's. The boy or man who has multiple sexual partners and strong sexual interest is a 'stud'; a similar girl or woman is a 'slut.' . . . The double standard is nurtured by cultures such as our own in which men dominate politics and the economy. Sexual access to women is part of the property system; men assert their high status by having sex with as many partners and as often as possible, whereas women keep themselves precious (and worthy of marriage) by saving themselves for the right man."

> **—Naomi B. McCormick,** *Sexual Salvation: Affirming Women's Sexual Rights and Pleasures*

What a Feminist Icon Said:

"A liberated woman is one who has sex before marriage and a job after."

—Gloria Steinem

Feminism's role in changing social mores by increasing the recognition of women's sexuality, bolstering its acceptance, and encouraging greater access to birth control is celebrated as a great triumph. They point out how women's sexuality was once seen as "dangerous" or potentially unhealthy, and highlight the benefits of women's increased sexual freedom.

We can all agree that everyone is better off when women (and men) recognize the healthy role that sex should play in their lives. Yet some feminists do much more than invite women to get in touch with their sexuality and understand better the role that society plays in shaping morality; they encourage women to engage in greater sexual experimentation.

Leading feminist icon Gloria Steinem summed up the feminist take on what it means to be a modern woman: "A liberated woman is one who has sex before marriage and a job after." In other words, if you don't have sex before marriage, you don't count as liberated.

In her book, *Slut! Growing up Female with a Bad Reputation*, feminist author Leora Tanenbaum explores the devastating impact that being labeled promiscuous can have on a woman's life and the variety of ways—many of which don't involve engaging in sexual activity—that a young woman can acquire the label of "slut."

No woman deserves to be tormented by her peers, but Tanenbaum reveals her poor opinion of women who fail to engage in sexual experimentation and associate sex with love. She highlights the work of one researcher who studied four hundred teenage girls who spent "thousands of hours planning for the first sex." Typically, these girls didn't experience much physical pleasure from intercourse and were "distraught" after the relationships failed. She summarizes what she sees as the problem:

> These girls' unrealistic expectations of fusing love and sex led
> directly to profound unhappiness.... Unlike these "true-love
> narrators," a small number of girls interviewed by Thompson
> kept romance and sex in healthy perspective. These girls...
> sought sexual pleasure as well as romance while maintaining
> an independent sense of themselves. They took responsibility
> by using contraception. And these girls had a good time. When
> relationships failed, they maintained their sense of humor and
> the outlook that there were always other guys.

In other words, it's a mistake for young women to take sex too seriously or to let an expectation of a loving relationship get intermingled with their sexual desires. Clearly, teenage girls who decide to become sexually active with their boyfriends based on the assumption that it will lead to marriage are often deluding themselves. They should be aware that most high school relationships break up, which is one reason they may want to avoid becoming sexually involved with their boyfriends since that may increase the heartbreak at the end of the relationship.

Tanenbaum's definition of a "healthy" attitude toward sex is one that's primarily physical and allows a woman to shrug off the loss of a lover. She goes on to contrast the boring lives that those who equate sex with love can expect with the vibrant, colorful lives enjoyed by sexually active women who forgo monogamy.

Some feminists have recognized that the new sexual ethics have had negative consequences for women. Feminist author Sally Cline laments how women have adopted the worst characteristics of men and refers to the modern, post-sexual revolution era as "The Genital Appropriation Era":

> What the Genital Appropriation Era actually permitted was
> more access to women's bodies by more men; what it actually
> achieved was not a great deal of liberation for women but a
> great deal of legitimacy for male promiscuity; what it actually

passed on to women was the male fragmentation of emotion from body, and the easily internalized schism between genital sex and responsible loving.[4]

Feminist writer Naomi Wolf echoed this sentiment in an article on Jessica Cutler. Wolf admits that the sexual revolution has been a double-edged sword, leaving women more sexually free but confused about sex's proper role:

> What is gained is they totally reject the double standard and believe they are entitled to sexual exploration and sexual satisfaction. The down-side is we've raised a generation of young women—and men—who don't understand sexual ethics like: Don't sleep with a married man; don't embarrass people with whom you had a consensual relationship. They don't see sex as sacred or even very important anymore. That's been lost. Sex has been commodified and drained of its deeper meaning.[5]

It's an important message for young women to hear from leaders of the feminist movement. Unfortunately, these kinds of statements are drowned out by a flood of contrary messages on college campuses, in popular culture, and in many women's studies texts and feminist writings. From those sources a young woman might reasonably conclude that she's falling down on her responsibility to be modern and liberated if she doesn't experiment with casual sex or views a physical relationship as appropriate only between a man and woman within the confines of marriage or a monogamous relationship.

Sexual freedom is not exactly liberating

Not all sexually experienced teens and young adults are happy with their decisions. Many report that they regret having had sex. A Kaiser Family

Oxymoron: Casual Sex

*C*asual sex. Who knew it could be so complicated? After all, the word "casual" carries with it an implication of carelessness and simplicity—but perhaps that's where the problems begin. As much as no-strings-attached action may be a spur-of-the-moment experience, we've come to realize that being careless can make casual sex a lot less fun for a girl, both physically and emotionally. That's why we urge you to think through it as completely as possible....This is one of the many reasons we wrote this book....

The bottom line: It feels good and, given the right situation, it makes you feel good about yourself.... And there's absolutely nothing wrong with that, sister. No way, no how.

The Happy Hook Up: A Single Girl's Guide to Casual Sex

Foundation/*Seventeen Magazine* (2003) survey found that more than six in ten sexually active teenage girls wished they had waited to have sex. Nearly four in ten of the sexually active girls specifically wished they had waited until they were older.[6]

The survey conducted by the National Campaign to Prevent Teen Pregnancy found an even higher level of regret among sexually active teens. Two-thirds wished they had waited longer before having sex—an increase from 2002 when 63 percent said they wished they had waited. Girls were more likely to regret having had sex than were boys: Nearly eight in ten girls and six in ten boys wish they had waited.[7]

This level of regret isn't surprising when you consider the role peer pressure plays in many teenagers' decisions to have sex. This is particularly true of girls. According to the Kaiser Family Foundation/*Seventeen Magazine* survey, more than nine out of ten girls strongly or somewhat agreed with the statement that "girls are often pressured to have sex before they are ready."

Feelings of regret and confusion don't end for women when they graduate from high school. Glenn and Marquardt highlight, in their report on the sex and dating culture on college campuses, the conflicting feelings that many young women express about these brief "relationships":

> Women said that after a hook up they often felt awkward and sometimes felt hurt. A number of them reported not knowing if the hook up would lead to anything else, which made them feel confused if they wanted something more from the encounter. At the same time, a number of women also reported feeling strong, desirable, and sexy after a hook up.[8]

The dissatisfaction these women experience isn't uncommon for those who engage in casual sex. In *Taking Sex Differences Seriously*, Steven Rhoads highlights the work of an anthropologist, John Townsend, who conducted in-depth interviews with forty medical students and fifty undergraduates, selected because they were "unusually open to casual

Your doctor might have to treat that color.

Sexual rules lead to sexual repression. Girls and women who shoehorn sex within the confines of adolescent romance describe their sexuality in shades of grey. Those who are sexually active yet refuse to commit to one boy, portray their sexuality—and, indeed, their entire lives—in vibrant color.

—**Leora Tanenbaum**, *Slut! Growing Up Female with a Bad Reputation* sex." Townsend found that, over time, these women tended to reject casual sex after experiencing three stages.

In the first stage, women viewed casual sex as an opportunity to test their attractiveness and didn't feel emotionally scarred by the experience. In the second stage, the women had trouble rectifying competing emotions: "they say that sex without emotion is okay, but they worry about the guy's intentions after intercourse because previous sexual encounters have not evolved into the desired relationships." In the final stage, women rejected casual sex in hopes of finding a relationship that would provide more emotional support and commitment from their partners.[9]

Both Townsend and Glenn and Marquardt note that women expressed frustration with their emotions, or blamed themselves, not for engaging in casual sex, but for feeling emotionally involved afterwards.[10] When reality didn't match feminist dogma, women assumed the problem was their own.

Regret about having too many sexual partners is common among women. A 1998 poll conducted by *Glamour* magazine reported that nearly half of the women interviewed (49 percent) wish they had slept with fewer men. Less than one in ten (7 percent) wish they'd had more partners.

Even cheerleaders for casual sex acknowledge that many women tend to regret these liaisons and must steel themselves against allowing emotions to spoil the fun. *The Happy Hook Up: A Single Girl's Guide to Casual Sex* includes a list of tips to "get your head in the game." Among the rules that must govern casual sex are to "understand that sex is not love"; "keep your emotions and your orgasms separate"; "make sure it's just sex"; "limit the encounters"; "keep yourself busy"; and "bond with the girls." Women are warned against engaging in casual sex with someone in whom they might possibly be interested for a real relationship.[11]

The authors warn that casual sex isn't for all women, because many can't successfully follow these rules. Yet even the women who participated in the "Happy Hookup Survey"—a sample likely to be far more comfortable with casual sex than the average woman—struggled with regret. Nearly nine in ten of the free-wheeling women surveyed admitted regretting having casual sex at one time.[12]

A biological aversion to casual sex

Our tenured women's studies professor undoubtedly would point out that the negative emotions women experience are a reaction to societal expectations. A feeling of shame isn't innate but a product of the patriarchal structure that has created an ideal of purity for women.

Societal expectations may contribute to some of the emotions women experience. But regardless of the source, young women deserve to understand that they might experience negative emotions after engaging in casual sex.

"Patriarchy" is just one possible source—and an unlikely one at that—of the emotional link between sex and love. For some, their religious faith says certain behavior is wrong. Human anthropology is another possible source: Sex with men unwilling to invest in the woman or any offspring almost certainly endangered a woman's chances for survival. As Townsend hypothesizes, "we possess unconscious emotional-motivation mechanisms that warn women via bad feelings when they engage in sexual behavior that would have been maladaptive in earlier evolutionary eras. Casual sex with men unwilling to invest in them or their offspring is a prime instigator of such negative feelings."[13]

In *Taking Sex Differences Seriously*, Rhoads explores how the physical differences between men and women shape their responses to sex. Women are more vulnerable to the physical consequences of sex, including pregnancy and disease (discussed in a later chapter). Women are also different hormonally than men, with the hormones that increase in men and women during puberty affecting them in different ways. Women react to these physical changes with an increased desire for "bonding" as well as an increased sex drive, while men have no greater desire to "get close." During this time period, teenage boys tend to want more time alone while girls seek greater companionship.[14] These hormonal differences help to explain why women have a more difficult time separating sexual activity from emotional responses.

Dr. Ian Kerner of *Be Honest—You're Not That Into Him Either* also singles out biological responses as a cause of women becoming seriously involved with men they don't really want to be with forever. Women tend to feel connected to a man after sleeping with him, in part, because of the release of hormones that accompanies sex, oxytocin and dopamine, which trigger emotions in women such as affection and attachment.

As a result, women end up wasting time with guys that they "really aren't that into." After a series of such relationships, some become anxious to marry due to their advancing age and end up "settling" for a man that they don't really desire. Alternatively, women may end up disappointed when a relationship fails to develop into anything beyond casual sex, even when that was all they had intended. It is a double-edged sword, and a sharp one emotionally.

The negative emotions women experience after casual sex also may be because, as unfair and frustrating as it may seem, men are more likely to pursue serious relationships with women who reserve sex for marriage or committed monogamy. Steven Rhoads highlights research that suggests men's attraction to chaste women may also have evolutionary roots:

Turn off your cell phones, ladies.

PIG

A modern woman is required to assign a higher place to her desire for autonomy than to her desire for connection. She is supposed to be tough enough to stand on her own two feet, without worrying about whether her partner in a one-night stand will ever call her again.

—Jennifer Roback Morse, *Smart Sex: Finding Life-Long Love in a Hook-Up World*

Men often prize promiscuous sex in the short term, but they want faithful wives. Through the ages, men with faithful mates have sired more children, and a taste for faithfulness will thus have been "naturally selected" for. If a man finds a woman hard to get, he will sense that she is more likely to be faithful after marriage.[15]

The benefits of serious sex

In *A Return to Modesty*, Wendy Shalit emphasizes just how unsexy casual sex really is. For women who embrace the ethic that sex is meaninglessly recreation, nothing remains erotic. Shalit summarizes their attitude as: *It's no big deal*.

Modesty and the discipline of reserving sex for true love, on the other hand, increase the sense that something very important is happening. That heightened importance makes modesty more erotic than the casual free-for-all celebrated as sexual liberation.

Young women overwhelmed by the coarse sexual climate and inundated with the message that casual sex is an important part of being a modern woman should consider some of women's real experiences. Many women regret casual sex, not just immediately, but also years later when they've married or finally found the love of their lives.

Of course, as will be discussed in more detail in chapter five, women face far more than emotional risks when it comes to casual sex. There are also significant physical risks that young women need to consider before engaging in casual sex.

From *Friends*:

Joey: Heh. Let me get this straight. He got you to beg to sleep with him. He got you to say he never has to call you again. And he got you thinking this is a great idea?

Phoebe: [*weakly*] Uh-huh.

Joey: This man is my God!

None of this is to suggest that all young women need to embrace abstinence until marriage nor does it require that society go back to the days of demonizing sexually active unmarried women. But young women should recognize the pitfalls of casual sex that often are hidden in our sex-saturated culture and consider the benefits of taking sex seriously.

Chapter Four

NOT EVERYONE IS DOING IT

 *N*ot all teenagers are sexually active and fewer young adults than you might think are racking up significant numbers of sexual partners. That's not the message you get from popular culture. If television or magazines geared toward women were any guide, you might assume that all teens and young adults are engaging numerous lovers. The message to parents is that there's no point in trying to discourage teenage children from having sex; at best encourage them to use contraception to limit the risk of pregnancy and disease.

In reality, parents play a huge role in shaping their children's attitudes and choices about sex. It's important for young women (and men) to know that not all of their peers are sexually active because the desire to "fit in" can have real influence on their behavior.

Popular culture's message to kids: just do it!

Sex education begins in elementary school throughout much of America today. Thongs are marketed to girls as young as seven. Magazines that cater to pre-teen audiences are filled with advice about sex and relationships. Teenage girls increasingly get breast implants—some as graduation presents from their parents.

Guess what?

- Television and movies often make it seem as though a teenage virgin is as rare as a unicorn.

- Surveys reveal that many teens are pretty conservative in their ideas about the role of sex and the importance of virginity.

- Parents have an important role to play in shaping teens' attitudes toward sex.

In youth culture, sex is nearly inescapable. Television and movies often make it seem as though a teenage virgin is as rare as a unicorn.

One recurring plot in the hit 1990s television show *Beverly Hills 90210* revolved around the character Donna Martin (played by Tori Spelling)—a virgin who initially aspired to wait until marriage. This incredibly old fashion sentiment caused endless problems for Donna in the *90210* world, and the audience waited to see when this last virgin would finally wise up and give in.

The message was a carryover from 1980s teen classics such as *Breakfast Club* and *Sixteen Candles*, in which the high school characters are loath to admit that they're still virgins. These movies are now staples or "the new classics" featured regularly on cable television networks like TNT.

In the last few years, television shows like *The O.C.* and *Dawson's Creek* have continued to feature torrid teen age love affairs, and lament the fate of those awkward or unlucky teens that haven't yet sealed the deal. The hit movie *American Pie* centered on four high school guys' quests to lose their virginities by senior prom. Graduating high school as virgins was a fate too terrible to contemplate.

At the Movies

"You realize we're all going to go to college as virgins. They probably have special dorms for people like us."

—**Jim**, *American Pie* (1999)

It isn't just in the movies and on television where virgins are made to seem as out of date as ruffled tuxedos and shoulder pads. Best-selling author and Harvard law student Ben Shapiro describes how he's been ridiculed as the "The Virgin Ben." Shapiro has written extensively about the over-sexualization of his generation—which he dubs the "porn generation"—and advocates abstinence, making him an easy target. Critics mock him as having had celibacy "thrust upon him" and that "not once is he ever going to get to have really good hot sweaty sex." In his most recent book, *Porn*

Generation, Shapiro notes that the ridicule he faces is a common experience for high schoolers and college students who abstain from sex:

> My own experience is representative of what many members of the porn generation endure in their own high schools and on their college campuses every day. We're forced to undergo this experience because, in the twisted view of the sex-obsessed moral relativists, abstinence before marriage is a demented way of life, and virginity itself is seen as a sort of strange plague. In a world where deviance is praised, purity is the new sin.

If actual virgins are exotic and repressed, it's nearly as bad for men and women who aren't regularly doing the deed. Valerie Frankel—whose columns appear in women's magazines such as *Mademoiselle*, *Redbook*, *Allure*, and *Self*—wrote a novel, *The Accidental Virgin*, which details the horror thirty-something Stacy feels when she realizes she hasn't had sex in almost a year. Stacy reads that if you go a whole year without sex, you will be "revirginized" and thus embarks on a week-long quest to avoid this sorry fate. She attempts to seduce her boss's twenty-year-old son, a delivery man, and several other acquaintances. She begins having a lesbian encounter with a coworker, and considers hiring a male escort to do the job.

Stacy lives in a glamorous New York world of sophisticated parties and fancy clothes, and her reaction to her predicament is depicted as perfectly normal: This heroine is the picture of a liberated woman who has seized control of her sex drive.

The applause for sexually free women isn't reserved just for adults and isn't limited to popular culture. Some feminists write with equal fervor about sexual freedom among younger women, including teens.

In *Listen Up: Voices from the Next Feminist Generation*, a book that purports to provide a voice and forum for young feminists, essayist Rebecca Walker (named by *Time* magazine as one of the fifty future leaders of America) describes her own sexual exploration, including losing her virginity at age eleven. She extols the importance of greater accept-ance of sexual liberation for young women (i.e., girls) and makes the case that sex should be seen as an opportunity for personal growth, not an expression of love for another person.

While Walker focuses on breaking societal taboos against premarital sex and sexual activity by the very young, she also tries to change the reader's view of what's normal. She tries to convince the reader that inter-course by an eleven-year-old is not only appropriate, but also common-place: "Shocking, right? Not really. Sex begins much earlier than most people think, and it is far more extensive."

Walker envisions a world where no one can or should encourage teens to forgo sexual intercourse. Instead, she argues that parents should help their children embark on this exploration and simply provide contracep-tion: "The question is not whether young women are going to have sex, for this is far beyond any parental or societal control. The question is rather, what do young women need to make sex a dynamic, affirming, safe and pleasurable part of our lives?"[1]

The message is that parents should just give up on urging sexual restraint for their daughters (and sons) after age eleven. It's no use; kids are going to do it anyway, so you may as well put them on the pill or hand them a box of condoms. Probably best to get ready to help raise your grandchildren—they may be coming sooner than you think.

Teens and young adults: not as sexually active as you—or they—might think

Contrary to Walker's declaration, teens actually tend to *over-estimate* how sexually active their peers are.

In 2003, the Kaiser Family Foundation and *Seventeen Magazine* sur-veyed boys and girls aged fifteen to seventeen about their sexual experi-ences and attitudes toward sex.[2] Of those interviewed, 32 percent

responded that they had had sexual intercourse—including 36 percent of the boys
and 28 percent of the girls. This is lower
than a survey completed by the Center for
Disease Control and Prevention (CDC). The
CDC found that 46.7 percent of high school
students had had sexual intercourse during
their lifetimes. Just 7.4 percent of students

A Book You're Not Supposed to Read

Porn Generation: How Social Liberalism Is Corrupting Our Future, by Ben Shapiro; Washington, D.C., Regnery Publishing, 2005.

surveyed—and 4.2 percent of the girls—experienced sex before the age
of thirteen.[3]

So while it's true that many high schoolers have had sex, it's important to recognize that a majority has not.

Most teens don't know this fact. A survey conducted by the National
Campaign to Prevent Teen Pregnancy found that teens routinely overestimate the number of their peers who are sexually active, with two-thirds
of the teenage girls surveyed agreeing with the statement that "most teens
my age have had sex."[4]

Similarly, the Kaiser Family Foundation/*Seventeen Magazine* survey
revealed that one in three teens overestimated the percentage of sexually active high schoolers compared to one in four who underestimated
this rate. Girls' perceptions were more skewed than boys: They were
twice as likely to overestimate as underestimate the percentage of sexually active teens.[5]

Sexually active students were even more prone to overestimate the
number of their peers who were sexually experienced: 56 percent said
that *80 percent* of their peers were sexually active. This is a significant
misperception if you assume that the CDC's estimate that just under half
of teenagers are sexually active is generally accurate. Only 10 percent of
sexually active teenagers underestimated the level of sexual activity.

This is very important because teens' perceptions of what's "normal"
influences their decisions. Sixty-two percent of sexually active teens

surveyed by *Seventeen Magazine* believed "many of their friends had already done it" and this influenced their decision to have sex.[6]

It's equally important for teenagers to know that, contrary to what they see on television and in movies, few of their friends—and even few of the twenty-somethings—are racking up numerous sexual partners. Only 11 percent of high school girls surveyed by the CDC reported having had

Getting "Rid" of Your Virginity— One Young Woman's Story

*I*t's a big deal–losing your virginity is supposed to be something you do when you're in love and its supposed to be special and society has created this stigma around it, but you talk to everyone and nobody lost their virginity in this perfect flowers and candles kind of way. Everyone's sucked. People were drunk, people didn't tell the guy they were a virgin, it wasn't perfect for anybody. So I started thinking about it more and more and more and I was like, "God, I just want to get it over with and not have to worry about it anymore." So when I was home over spring break...I hooked up with this guy I know from home and asked him to take my virginity, so that was that.

[Now] I feel strangely emotionless about it. It's liberating because I don't have to worry about it....at least he knew I was a virgin...I wasn't drunk, another plus. I remember it...I thought about it a long time....It would be really nice to have a flower and candles virginity losing, it would be really nice to be in love—I've never been in love—that would be great, I'm jealous of people who get to experience that, but I guess I just feel like I'm settling a little bit...but it's not like I'm missing out on something that everyone else gets.

—A twenty-year-old college junior,
interviewed by author

four or more sexual partners.[7] This number may be high, but it still represents a small minority of teens.

A study of sexually active people in their twenties found that just 31 percent of men and 20 percent of women had more than one sexual partner in the past year.[8]

Furthermore, a 1997 survey of college students provided some pretty disturbing statistics: nearly half had had a one-night stand, 43 percent had cheated on a steady partner, and 36 percent had had sex with someone they didn't like. These numbers aren't exactly encouraging, but they can be looked at from a "glass half full" perspective: More than half of college students *hadn't* had a one night stand. This suggests that the image portrayed on television and in movies—of women and men changing sexual partners as rapidly as they change clothes—doesn't reflect reality for the majority of women or men.

Teens who want to mimic their peers also should be aware that many of their sexually active friends think they made a mistake. As discussed in the last chapter, teen age girls who became sexually active wished overwhelmingly they had waited until they were older.

More alarming is the number of young girls that confess to undesired intercourse. Among teen girls aged fifteen to nineteen, who have had sexual intercourse, 24 percent described their first time as "voluntary and unwanted" and 7 percent as "involuntary." Therefore, teenage girls seeking to "fit in" not only should adjust their perceptions of the number of their peers who are sexually active, but also account for the fact that more than three in ten of their sexually-active peers didn't want or didn't voluntarily have sex.

Most teens think being a virgin is positive

Surveys reveal that many teens, even those who are sexually active, are pretty conservative in their ideas about the role of sex and the importance of virginity. Ninety-five percent of girls and 89 percent of boys strongly or somewhat agreed with the statement that, "I think being a virgin in high school is a good thing." When asked, "At what age do you personally think it is OK for someone to lose his or her virginity?" a majority responded with "eighteen or older."

Strikingly, one in four *volunteered* that virginity should be maintained until marriage. More than one-third of those who had not yet experienced intercourse planned on waiting until marriage and another four in ten planned on waiting for a committed relationship. Even among those who were sexually active before age eighteen, 17 percent volunteered that marriage is the appropriate time to begin sexual relations, and most thought it was best to be over eighteen or married.[9]

Given these facts, it's sad that women feel pressure to become sexually active to avoid a perceived stigma associated with being a "virgin." One young woman interviewed for this book detailed the burden that her virginity became and how she had decided to get "rid" of it. She stressed that she was happy in general with her decision—but she seemed to be trying to convince herself that she shouldn't be disappointed that it lacked the romance she had clearly wanted.

Parents have an important role to play

A primary finding of the research conducted by the National Campaign to Prevent Teen Pregnancy is that parents have an important role to play in shaping teens' attitudes toward sex.

Parents tend to discount their own importance in influencing the attitudes of their children: Nearly half (45 percent) of teens ranked parents as most influential in their decisions about sex—which made them more influential than any other group. Just three out of ten teens (31 percent) said that their friends were most influential, followed by religious leaders (7 percent), teachers and sex educators (6 percent), and the media (4 percent).

Few parents recognize how important their opinions are to their children. Nearly half (48 percent) believed that their children's friends had the greatest influence, compared to just three in ten (32 percent) who thought that parents had the greatest impact.[10]

Conclusion

Knowing that they're not alone in never having been sexually active can help young men and women avoid feeling like outcasts because they're virgins. It can encourage some teenagers and young adults to put off sex and make them more comfortable with their decision to abstain since there are considerable physical and emotional risks, especially for women, if they engage in casual sex.

Chapter Five

THE RISKS OF SAFE SEX

Sex education can start as early as elementary school for America's children. In addition to learning the birds and the bees, sex education classes teach students the many benefits of contraception. Teens are encouraged to practice safe sex whenever the time comes, particularly through the use of condoms. This message is echoed on college campuses and in popular culture geared toward twenty-somethings: Condoms are the responsible way to avoid the unwanted consequences of casual sex.

Certainly condoms are a useful tool for reducing the risk of unwanted pregnancy and sexually transmitted diseases (STDs)—but they're no get-out-of-STD free device. There are many sexually transmitted diseases that condoms—even when properly used—don't necessarily prevent from spreading.

The fallibility of condoms helps explain why, even with the increased awareness about the potential for STDs and the increased reported use of contraception, the prevalence of infection among teens and young adults has continued to climb. Young women are at particular risk for contracting and sustaining lasting damage from STDs.

Young women need to know that condoms aren't fool proof in preventing the spread of STDs. Some health professionals are reticent to give

Guess what?

- Liberal sex education courses leave out important information.

- Young women, liberated from the fear of unwanted pregnancy because of contraception, may be engaging in more sexual activity leading to sexually transmitted diseases.

- Condoms, while reducing many health risks, are of limited utility in protecting against several sexually transmitted diseases of serious concern to women.

youngsters this message since they fear they'll stop using protection altogether, but young men and women deserve the truth about an issue critical to their health.

Sex education—more than the birds and the bees

Most parents expect sex education to provide adolescents with the basic facts about reproduction and contraception. In truth, sex education courses today often serve as forums to instill liberal morals and a feminist world view in students.

A good example is the Sexuality Information and Education Council of the United States (SEICUS), a national organization that receives financial support from American taxpayers through the CDC. SEICUS advocates for much more than just comprehensive sex education, it also fights for abortion rights and "social justice."

SIECUS's School Health Project is designed to help state and local health and education departments provide "high quality, culturally appropriate education designed to prevent HIV, STDs, and unintended pregnancy among teens." In addition to providing training seminars for educators, creating materials for distribution to teens, and reaching out to community groups, SEICUS develops guidelines for what should be taught in sex education from kindergarten to twelfth grade.

SIECUS's "Guidelines for Comprehensive Sexuality Education" focuses on educating students about six key concepts: human development, relationships, personal skills, sexual behavior, sexual health, and society and culture. It breaks down the messages they believe are appropriate for students based on age.

Among the developmental messages deemed appropriate for those ages five through eight is "both boys and girls have body parts that feel good when touched"; "vaginal intercourse—when a penis is placed inside a vagina—is the most common way for a sperm and egg to join";

and "touching and rubbing one's own genitals to feel good is called masturbation." By level two—ages nine through twelve—students are learning about bisexuality and abortion.

Some parents reading this may believe that these messages are appropriate for children at these ages; however, many parents are horrified. As a result of the conflicting views about what kids should or shouldn't learn about sex at school, the content of sex education courses has become a political battleground. Conservatives have attempted to shift the dialogue in many public schools from emphasizing contraception to emphasizing abstinence. Supporters of abstinence-only education argue that sex education encourages more experimentation. Those, like SEICUS, who oppose abstinence-only education claim that it leaves students ignorant about how to protect themselves and more likely to engage in risky behaviors.

The Politically Correct Attitude Toward Sex

"As long as I'm safe, what the hell?"

—Feminist writer, **Anastasia Higginbotham** in an essay in *Listen Up: Voices from the Next Feminist Generation*

The abstinence movement has been the subject of much ridicule from liberal groups. In July 2005, the Washington state chapter of the abortion rights group, NARAL Pro-Choice America, held a "Screw Abstinence Party." According to this fundraiser's invitation, guests were treated to entertainment by "Pork Filled Players—Seattle theatre's hottest sketch comedy group performs a sex ed class for adults"; and, "Toys in Babeland—Seattle's sleaze-free, sex-positive purveyors of adult toys offer tips on 'Sexy Safer Sex.'"

Ridiculing abstinence is politically correct, but it tells us nothing about its effectiveness. Some studies suggest that abstinence programs are very successful in encouraging students to forgo sexual intercourse and decrease the prevalence of STDs and unwanted pregnancy.[1] Other research has been critical of the content of abstinence programs, claiming that they use alarmist statistics about the failure rate of condoms and prevalence of STDs to scare kids into abstaining from sex.[2]

This debate about what should be taught in sex education classes in public schools is an advertisement for why we need school choice, or policies that give parents more options and greater control over where their children attend school. There wouldn't have to be a one-size-fits-all solution to sex education if parents were free to choose a school for their child that reflected their personal beliefs; instead, parents are stuck with their local public schools.

Regardless of where one comes out in this debate, all should be able to agree that it's important for teenagers to be aware of the potential for contracting an STD and the limitations of condoms in preventing their spread. The SEICUS materials talk extensively about various forms of contraception. As a part of teaching the topic "contraception," level three students (twelve to fifteen) are supposed to learn:

- Some methods of contraception, such as withdrawal, are not as effective as others.
- Some methods of contraception, such as condoms, can also prevent the transmission of STDs/HIV.
- The most effect methods of contraception, such as the Pill, injection, and the birth control patch, do not help prevent the transmission of STDs/HIV.
- Couples who want to reduce their risk for both pregnancy and STDs/HIV need to use male or female condoms along with another effective method of contraception.
- Any method of contraception, in order to be effective in preventing pregnancy and STDs/HIV, must be used consistently and correctly.

These students are also told, as a part of the "sexually transmitted disease" topic, that "Proper use of latex condoms, along with water-based lubricants, can greatly reduce, but not eliminate the chance of getting an STD."

This leaves out a lot of information for students. SEICUS has recommended detailed discussions among students about the important, healthy role that sexuality plays in people's lives, the need for acceptance and understanding of life choices made by others, and the importance of creating your own values. Limits in our ability to prevent the spread of STDs, some of which can have lasting health consequences for these students, deserve as much, if not more, emphasis.

At least formal sex education classes often acknowledge that condoms are an imperfect method of disease prevention. The rest of youth culture tends to leave this message out entirely, celebrating sex so long as it's done "responsibly."

Condoms' great P.R.

The idea that sex is costless so long as it's "safe" is sacred dogma on many campuses—with "safe" usually defined as sex with condoms. Condoms are championed at America's colleges (and high schools), and student health centers and associations sometimes provide them for free.[3]

One young feminist writer summed up the sentiments of many on the importance of "safe" sex. She celebrates her rejection of the cultural prohibitions surrounding female promiscuity, discounting any physical risks since she practices "safe" sex: "The only other reason that could prevent me from embracing my bisexual identity is the implication to others that I might be easy. Ain't no might about it. I am easy. But, as long as I'm safe, what the hell?"[4]

A Book You're Not Supposed to Read

Epidemic: How Teen Sex Is Killing Our Kids, Meg Meeker, M.D., Washington, DC, LifeLine Press, 2002.

Women's magazines also contribute to the widespread misperception that casual sex is safe as long condoms are used. *Marie Claire* featured an article on the activities of a subculture of people engaging in anonymous group sex. The article mentions how participants are "opening themselves up to the threat of STDs," highlighting how many participants fail to use condoms.[5]

In two interviews with group sex participants, both proudly boast of using condoms during their encounters. One man brags, "I always take condoms with me—and insist on using them." Another woman explains, "Some nights, I had sex with up to ten people. But I always used condoms."[6] Condoms are depicted as a get-out-of-STD-free card. As if, because they use condoms, their actions are somehow responsible.

Admittedly, it's *preferable* that group sex participants use condoms—but the politically correct myth that condoms wipe away the risks of casual sex is just that—a myth.

Women's biological vulnerability

The most well-known vulnerability that women face from sexual intercourse is unwanted pregnancy. And even though rates of teenage pregnancy have declined, many women continue to become pregnant before they're ready.

According to the National Campaign to Prevent Teen Pregnancy, one in three women get pregnant at least once before age twenty.[7] An estimated eight in ten teen pregnancies are unplanned and out of wedlock.[8] About 30 percent of teen pregnancies end in abortion, which indicates that more than 250,000 teens have a pregnancy terminated each year.[9] Regardless of one's position on the legality of abortion, it seems reasonable to assume that no woman *wants* to undergo the procedure and thus these numbers are cause for concern.

Although high, these statistics are in some sense good news. Rates of teen pregnancy have dropped considerably since 1990—a fact celebrated by many health professionals and politicians. Many experts attribute most of this decline to increased use of contraceptives.

But even as the rate of unwanted pregnancy has fallen by nearly 30 percent since its peak in 1990, the number of STD infections has continued to rise. Each year approximately ten million individuals in the fifteen to twenty-four age group contract an STD, which means that of those who are sexually active, an estimated one in three will contract an STD before age twenty-four.[10]

For example, the rate of infection of genital herpes grew 30 percent since 1970, with the largest increase occurring in young teens. According to the CDC, forty-five million Americans over age twelve—or one out of five of the total adolescent and adult population—are infected with genital herpes. Those who are infected can look forward to a life time of periodic outbreaks of sores in the genital region.[11]

The human papillomavirus (HPV) has received increased attention in recent years due to a growing awareness of the virus's relationship with cervical cancer. HPV is the name of a collection of more than one hundred different viruses, only some of which are sexually transmitted. Most of these viruses are not associated with any symptoms and disappear on their own. Others cause genital warts which are treatable. However, some strains of HPV can have serious consequences, such as potentially leading to cancer, particular cervical cancer, in women. The CDC estimates that nearly half of all sexually active people will acquire at HPV infection during their lives.

Chlamydia infections are the most common sexually transmitted diseases and the diagnosed incidences of chlamydia has skyrocketed during the last twenty years. The CDC cautions that this higher rate of diagnosis may in part be good news—the increase could be attributable to better screening and more treatment, not just to an increase in the rate of contraction. Diagnosing chlamydia is particularly important since while it's treatable with antibiotics, left untreated it can result in pelvic inflammatory disease, which can cause infertility and other complications.[12]

Regardless of whether the rates of infection have climbed or have always been this high, this disease affects too many young women today. In fact, chlamydia is most common among women in the fifteen to twenty-four age group: in 2003, 2.5 percent of women in this age group were diagnosed with chlamydia.

The truth is "STDs are not gender-neutral"; women are far more likely than straight men to contract an STD.[13] A woman is eight times as likely to get HIV and four times more likely to get gonorrhea from one act of intercourse than is a man. Women are also more likely to have permanent damage from STDs, such as infertility and cancers. Yet, only one-third of women are aware of their greater vulnerability to contracting an STD.[14]

Of course, sexually transmitted diseases have more than just physical consequences. They also can be emotionally devastating, particularly for young people. Dr. Meg Meeker, author of the book *Epidemic: How Teen Sex Is Killing Our Kids*, details how all patients diagnosed with the lifelong disease of herpes experience a sense of loss and grieve while coming to terms with their illness, but she emphasizes that the diagnosis is particularly devastating to already insecure teenagers, often leading to depression and loss of self esteem.[15]

Is safe sex making kids less safe?

Some researchers believe that the increased awareness and availability of contraceptives have fueled the rise of sexually transmitted diseases. Young women, liberated from fear of the most immediate negative outcome from sexually intercourse—unwanted pregnancy—may be engaging in more sexual activity leading to the increase in STDs. Dr. Meeker sums up the relationship thus: "The very contraceptives that have made the teenage birthrate go down have also made casual sex easier than ever, thus making the STD rate simultaneously rocket up."[16]

In addition, once a teen has sex, it becomes much easier to do it again. As a result, teens end up engaging more partners and undertaking more risky behaviors. Not surprisingly, the younger a girl becomes sexually active the more likely she is to have numerous partners and the greater her chances of contracting an STD.

Rx: Advice from a doctor

*T*wenty years ago, I wouldn't have hesitated to prescribe oral contraceptives to teenage girls. In fact, any form of birth control was fine with me, as long as the patient used it consistently. As a young doctor swept away by the message of "safe" sex, I didn't know any better....

But today, I think long and hard about prescribing birth control pills or Depo-Provera to kids because this puts them in such grave danger of contracting at STD. In giving a girl birth control that I know will protect her from pregnancy, am I inadvertently encouraging her to pick up a sexually transmitted disease?

And if you might ask, "What about condoms?" read on. We place far too much trust in those slim packets of latex and lambskin. In most cases, the chances of condoms preventing STDs is almost as thin as the condoms themselves.

        —Dr. Meg Meeker, pediatrician and author of *Epidemic: How Teen Sex Is Killing Our Kids*

The limitations of condoms

Condoms, while reducing the risks of the transmission of many STDs, are of limited utility in protecting against several STDs of serious concern to women. A 2001 report by the National Institute of Allergy and Infectious Diseases found that condoms didn't reduce the likelihood of contracting the HPV.[17] The CDC notes the limitations of condoms in preventing the spread of genital ulcer diseases, such as genital herpes and syphilis, since infections can be present in skin not covered by a condom.[18] Condoms were found to be most effective in preventing HIV/AIDS, reducing the likelihood of transmission by approximately 85 percent per incident of intercourse—not bad, perhaps, but far from perfectly "safe."[19]

Condoms reduce the spread of disease only when used consistently and effectively. Unfortunately, teenagers tend to use condoms sporadically. A 1997 study of high school girls found that just about half had used a condom when they last had intercourse.[20] Once teens become involved in a sexual relationship, they are more likely to become lazy about using condoms. They have had sex without getting pregnant and without contracting an STD (at least that they know of), so they become less worried about the potential consequences of sex and are more likely to take risks.[21] This is one potential explanation for the finding that older teens (age eighteen and nineteen) were less likely to use condoms than younger teens (fifteen to seventeen).[22]

To be sure, it's far better to reduce the risk of transmission of these diseases than to take no precautions at all, so it's important for sexually active young adults to use condoms. But statements like "As long as I'm safe, what the hell?"[23] irresponsibly imply that sex is worry-free and just another recreational activity, as long as precautions are taken. Young Americans deserve to know the facts about the limits of condoms so they don't unknowingly take risks with their health.

Chapter Six

MEN AREN'T THE ENEMY

*V*iolence against women—whether it's domestic violence, rape, or other forms of assault—is a significant problem in the United States. All women need to educate themselves and take precautions to reduce the risk of being a victim.

Women also should recognize that such events are aberrations, completely inconsistent with healthy relationships. Unfortunately, this is often not the message that feminists and popular culture give to young women. Feminists often imply that men *in general* are hazardous to women's health and that violence against women is inescapable. Heterosexuality itself is cast as fraught with peril, emotionally and physically, for women.

Women should know the true facts about the prevalence of violence in our society, not the inflated statistics that feminists often repeat to suggest that violence against women is unavoidable. Although too many women are still victims, crime rates have actually dropped considerably during the last decade. It's also important to remember that violence affects both genders. In fact, men are far more likely to be victims of violent crime than are women.

A fact-based understanding of the prevalence of violence is the best way for women to protect themselves and their families.

Guess what?

- Women should know the true facts about the prevalence of violence in our society, not the inflated statistics that feminists often repeat.

- Feminists have unhelpfully conflated the actual experience of being assaulted with the mere potential for violence.

- By equating all men with a small minority of criminals, the problem of violence against women seems overwhelmingly large.

Danger: men among us

Women's studies textbooks often paint a picture of women under siege in American society. *Issues in Feminism: An Introduction to Women's Studies* describes women's relationship with men in these bleak terms:

> Feminists generally agree: Women are the victims of male violence. Such violence is an integral part of the gender system; it is largely sanctioned and reinforced by social institutions— the courts, the media, the economic system, religions, and others; it has an agenda, a goal—the control of women by men through fear.[1]

In this view, women's relationships with men are driven by the threat of violence. Women live in fear of ubiquitous male predators and so must seek protection from other men. It's the perfect set up to keep women completely subservient—at least from the point of view of a radical feminist.

We're all victims of violence

Feminists have unhelpfully conflated the actual experience of being assaulted with the mere potential for violence. It's under this calculus that all women are victims, even if we never actually experience an attack.

Consider this passage written by another young feminist author in the compilation, *Listen Up*, in which she describes her reaction to seeing *The Accused*. In this 1988 movie, the female lead (played by Jody Foster) is gang raped and then faces a torturous courtroom battle, during which she's accused of having "asked for it" by dressing provocatively and drinking at a bar:

> I recall an incident in which my friends and I discussed going to see *The Accused*. . . . I left the movie theater the following

weekend in tears, completely traumatized (scarred, in fact). I spent the next two days in exactly the same condition, crying for that woman, crying for myself and convinced that I would inevitably find myself pinned to a table by hovering, raping, evil men. My fear of rape and of men culminated in frequent nightmares about incest, murder and, of course, more rape. The problem was not that I suffered an abusive childhood or bad luck, because I didn't.... It was simply that I was born a girl in a society that devalues women and girls. Bam. That easy.[2]

It's this image of men that's reflected in the marquee feminist movie, *Thelma and Louise*. Each man that the heroines encounter exemplifies a different aspect of the abuse women suffer at the hands of men: a rapist attacks Thelma after she dances with him; Thelma's unfaithful, domineering husband seeks to control her every move; a seemingly attractive man (well, definitely attractive in that he's played by a young Brad Pitt, but he initially comes off as a good guy too) woos Thelma but ends up stealing all her money after she sleeps with him; Louise's boyfriend breaks into a fit of violence even while preparing to propose to her; a crass truck driver repeatedly harasses the women during their journey; and even the police detective, who is offered as a potential protector/savior, laughs with Thelma's husband and the other porn-reading police officers, and is ultimately unable to protect these women. Famously, the movie ends with the two heroine-victims clutching hands and driving off a cliff.

Lifetime television network propagates this view with a seemingly endless supply of made-for-TV movies in which the leading lady faces a constant threat of abuse from men who prey upon her. Scrolling through the movie titles and synopses on *Lifetime's* line up, the paranoid woman will find plenty of fodder for her fear.

Admittedly, television and movies generally dramatize life's events and focus on the most horrific stories. *ER* episodes rarely revolve around doctors confronting a stream of patients with flu symptoms and minor injuries—although no doubt such mundane ailments are the majority of cases that end up in the emergency room.

But *Lifetime* purports to bring women real information about the threats they face in their own lives. For example, the channel's website contains a page with the headline: "OUR LIFETIME COMMITMENT: STOP VIOLENCE AGAINST WOMEN." Among the alarming statistics that *Lifetime* cites is "One out of every four women on college campuses has been a victim of rape or attempted rape."[3]

Lifetime is certainly not alone in offering this alarming statistic as evidence of the pervasiveness of violence against women. Ask the average female college student the likelihood of a woman being the victim of a rape, and she will usually respond "one in four." As will be discussed later in this chapter, this statistic has a dubious origin, but its wide acceptance influences how women view men and relationships.

Redefining violence against women

What constitutes "violence" against women has been redefined in recent years. Sexual harassment laws have made off-color jokes and inappropriate comments not just brutish behavior, but crimes against women. The term "sexual harassment" isn't reserved for truly offensive instances where women are subjected to actual hostile threats and persecution. It has been used to refer to trivial office banter, displaying a picture of a loved one, or comments meant to compliment a coworker.

The definition of rape has become similarly diffuse. The term was once reserved for when women (or men) were forced into sex by use of physical aggression or threats. Now "rape" is sometimes used to describe very different circumstances, such as when a woman drinks alcohol, agrees to intercourse, but regrets it later.

These trends sow confusion and, in some ways, cheapen the genuine suffering endured by victimized women. Real instances of violence are horrific and completely inconsistent with healthy sexuality and functional relationships. They are not the norm. By equating all men with a

Lifetime Television's Line Up of Fear

Here are a few examples from Lifetime Television's listings of movies of how women are threatened by men:

Sin and Redemption (1994): "A young woman from a small college town is raped and becomes pregnant. She is afraid to tell anyone and unwittingly marries her rapist. The truth is revealed years later when their daughter falls ill and is in need of a kidney donor, and he is a perfect match."

Student Seduction (2003): "Christie Dawson wanted to be the kind of teacher that her students could always count on, the 'cool' teacher capable of inspiring young minds to actually want to learn chemistry. But after a pupil's crush on her spirals out of control, turns into obsession and he sexually assaults her, Christie is no longer sure she knows how to be both a teacher and a friend. Suddenly, her colleagues, neighbors and even her husband are pointing fingers in her direction and wondering how she could have crossed the line and tempted a high school student. Will she be able to prove her innocence?"

Without Her Consent (1990): "When a small-town girl heads to Los Angeles, the first friend she makes winds up date-raping her. And she isn't his first victim. See how this strong woman brings this sexual predator to justice."

Available at http://www.lifetimetv.com/movies/archive/index.html

small minority of criminals, the problem of violence against women seems overwhelmingly large; progress becomes impossible.

Forget men?

Individual young women warned away from men may wonder what alternative they have. Some women's studies textbooks suggest an alternative. They challenge students to examine their sexual preferences and to explore the possibility that they're not hard-wired to prefer the opposite sex. As one such textbook would have it, women are the victim of "heterosexual bribery":

> Such bribery revolves around "the dangerous fantasy that if you are good enough, pretty enough, sweet enough, quiet enough, teach the children to behave, hate the right people, and marry the right man, then you will be allowed to co-exist with patriarchy in relative peace" (Lorde 1984, 119). In any case our socialization as females widely inculcates beliefs such as these, namely, that straight white middle-class femininity is in our best interest.[4]

While another textbook, though celebrating the progress feminism has made in helping to "free women's sexual behavior from its traditional constraints," laments that the continued presumption of heterosexuality continues to "blind people to other possibilities for human sexual feeling and practice."[5]

Who's Afraid of Women's Studies highlights the work of feminist theorists who argue that even if we accept the idea that some women are innately heterosexual, women ought to be more aware of their "lesbian potential," and that "if lesbians were visible in an ordinary, casual, taken-for-granted way....It may be that heterosexuality would not occur to women as a viable way of living!"[6]

It's defensible for women's studies programs to cover lesbianism and challenge students to consider how societal expectations shape relationships and self-identity. However, it's curious that while most women's studies texts present very bleak depictions of heterosexuality, lesbianism receives a glowingly positive review:

> We may have much to learn from lesbian love and sex. As women loving women because they are women, lesbians point out that they are in a special position with regard to liberating female sexuality. Free of the heterosexual politics of the usual gender-based roles and prescriptions, more positive and self-affirming as women, more acutely aware of the needs of their partners . . . lesbian women contend that they are more able to discover and express authentic female sexuality than their heterosexual counterparts. Although lesbian couples share the conflicts of any two people in an intimate relationship, the experiences of many lesbian couples have valuable implications for creating nonexploitive relationships.[7]

Of the thirty-six essays in *Listen Up*, not one contains positive images of sexuality within a heterosexual, monogamous relationship. There are several essays on lesbianism, a few that celebrate promiscuity and sexual liberation, and numerous articles dealing with sexual violence against women by men. One author focuses on her struggle to reconcile her various identities as an "educated, married, monogamous, feminist, Christian, African-American mother," but her husband and marriage remain in the background and there is certainly no discussion of their sex life. Sex and sexuality pervade the writing, but healthy, monogamous heterosexual sex is ignored.

Feminist groups and other supporters of the gay rights movement generally argue that sexuality is innate—that some women are born lesbians and that homosexuality isn't a chosen behavior. To be consistent, one should also read that heterosexual women have to be true to themselves by pursuing relationships with members of the opposite sex.

Given the reality that most women are heterosexual and see building a happy monogamous relationship with a man as an important goal, women's studies programs should offer a more balanced picture of the dangers women face.

Violence against women *and* men

Before discussing the highly emotional topic of violence against women, the good news is that women are much less likely to be the victim of a violent crime than they were even a decade ago. The percentage of women who were the victim of a violent crime—including homicide, rape, robbery, and both simple and aggravated assault—dropped by more than half during the past ten years. The percentage for men has also dropped precipitously.

One often hears the phrase "violence against women," but rarely, if ever, the words "violence against men." Yet men continue to be much more likely than women to be the victims of a violent crime. Although violence against men has fallen during recent decades, men were almost 40 percent more likely than women to be the victim of violent crime in 2003, and 3.4 times as likely to be murdered in 2002.[8]

Of course, men also disproportionately commit violent crimes: Men were ten times as likely to commit homicide as were women in 2002, according to the Department of Justice. But these statistics conflict with the common notion that women are disproportionately the target of male violence. Male-on-male homicides accounted for nearly two-thirds of all cases, while male-on-female cases accounted for just over one-fifth. One in ten homicides was perpetrated by women-on-men; female-on-female homicides are the most infrequent, accounting for just 2 percent of all homicides.

One likely reason for the perception that women are disproportionately victims of violence is that women are often victims in cases that involve intimates. Nearly one third of female murder victims were murdered by a spouse, ex-spouse, or boyfriend/girlfriend, compared to just 5 percent of male victims. Women further accounted for nearly two-thirds of those murdered by intimates while men committed nearly two-thirds of such murders. Murders in which the parties know and are involved with each other can be presented more dramatically, and so received a disproportionate share of media attention. Such crimes may seem more terrifying since they involve the unthinkable idea of being killed by someone you know and may love, instead of just being in the wrong place at the wrong time.

Women also account for more than 80 percent of all sex-related murders, which tend to receive a great deal of media and public interest. In contrast, more than 90 percent of drug and gang related victims are men, which attracts far less interest. The public appears to discount the murders that occur between gang members and drug dealers, since those involved seem culpable for associating themselves with unsavory and illegal activities.

Crimes against women may also receive more focus from the public out of a traditional sense of chivalry. Society is more tolerant of violence between men, who are perceived as better able to defend themselves;

Wardrobe malfunction or fourth-degree sexual assault?

Super Bowl Sunday ended up a great day for fans of football, television commercials, popular music, live entertainment and, as it turns out, fourth-degree sexual assault. The stunt/accident/malfunction (or whatever you choose to name it) forced on millions of unsuspecting viewers by Justin Timberlake and Janet Jackson was a remarkably realistic dramatization of sexual violence rivaled only by online pushers of rape on the Internet.

Maggie Thurs, "Fallout from Breastgate: Sexual Assault as Entertainment," *San Francisco Chronicle*, February 11, 2004.

violence against women, who are generally perceived as weaker and more vulnerable, is more disturbing.

Ultimately, the reasons and disparities in the incidence of violence matter less than the importance of recognizing that both men and women are victims and our goal should be to reduce *all* violence, irrespective of gender.

Domestic violence or wife beating?

The perception that women are disproportionately victims is especially pronounced when it comes to discussions about domestic violence. Domestic violence is often described as "wife beating," as if all instances of domestic violence revolve around abuse within a married couple with the husband as the perpetrator.

Research into domestic violence reveals that violence is more evenly distributed than one might expect. Women and men are equally likely to act out violently in a relationship. The difference is men are much more likely to inflict serious harm on their partners. One study found that women were six times more likely than men to seek medical care due to a marital fight. According to the Department of Justice, women accounted for 84 percent of domestic violence injuries.

As author Cathy Young summarized in a report on domestic violence:

> Approximately half of all couple violence is mutual, with women initiating violence as well as striking in self-defense. When only one partner is abusive, it is just as likely to be the woman as it is to be the man. This does not mean that the affects of domestic violence are distributed equally. Women are much less likely to inflict lasting damage on a victim. One study found that women account for about two-thirds of injuries from domestic violence and women are more than twice as likely as men to be killed by a spouse of partner.[9]

In couples where abuse is severe, men account for three-quarters of the primary aggressors. Given the rhetoric surrounding domestic violence, it may surprise some that women are the primary aggressor in one out of four severely abusive couples and that men suffer 16 percent of all domestic violence injuries.

Domestic violence is a serious problem, and in order to craft policies and procedures to reduce the incidence of violence, it's important to recognize that women are not always passive victims in the relationships. They also can be aggressors.

Is marriage to blame?

Super Bowl Sunday is America's pseudo holiday. This most-watched TV event is an occasion for families and co-workers to get together, eat snacks, drink beer, and watch football; sounds innocent enough. But in 1993, the Super Bowl assumed a darker identity: the number one day for violence against women. Men, pumped up with testosterone and beer after watching the big game, were libel to snap and beat their wives—or so the story went.

Christina Hoff Sommers chronicles how, that year, despite the fact that the activists later admitted that they had no data to back up the claim that abuse increased on Super Bowl Sunday, NBC aired a public service announcement on the problem of domestic violence during the big game.[10] The media and public accepted this baseless claim without question because it fits the stereotypes about domestic violence. In scanning the reporting surrounding that incident, one such stereotype becomes clear: It's not just men who beat women; overwhelmingly, it's "husbands" who beat "wives."[11]

Researchers, public officials, and the media often lump all domestic violence cases into the terminology of wife battery, implying that marriage itself is associated or even responsible for these terrible incidents.

From researchers who title papers on violence "The Marriage License as Hitting License" to public officials who launch campaigns to arrest "violent husbands," the language of marriage is used to discuss domestic violence as if it were a problem that only exists between those who've vowed to stay together always.[12]

Linda Waite and Maggie Gallagher take on the myth that "Marriage Is A Hitting License" in their book, *The Case for Marriage*. They highlight how researchers commonly implicate marriage in domestic abuse situations:

> Even highly respected researchers, well aware that domestic violence is not confined to wives, tend to use wife abuse and domestic violence interchangeably, a linguist practice that in itself suggests that marriage puts women at heightened risk.... Domestic violence is perhaps the only area in which social scientists causally use the term husband to mean any or all of the following: the man one is married to, the man one used to be married to, the man one lives with, the man one is merely having sex with, and/or the man one used to have sex with.[13]

With an estimated 188,000 women battered each year, there's no doubt that domestic violence, or intimate partner abuse, against women in this country is a very significant problem.[14] But is marriage really to blame?

Research suggests that married women are *less* likely to be victims of violence than those who are divorced, separated, or unmarried but cohabitating with men. Waite and Gallagher studied the data collected in the National Crime Victimization Survey and found that two-thirds of attacks on women considered "intimate violence" (which means that attacks from friends or acquaintances are excluded) were not committed by husbands. Similarly, ex-spouses, boyfriends, or ex-boyfriends were responsible for 21 percent of rapes compared to the 5 percent committed by husbands (acquaintances, friends, or other relatives were responsible for more than half of rapes).[15]

Violence within marriage certainly exists. But young women contemplating their future relationships should understand that violence infests only a minority of marriages. Less than 2 percent of wives and 1 percent of husbands are subjected to an episode of violence that results in physical injury in a year.[16]

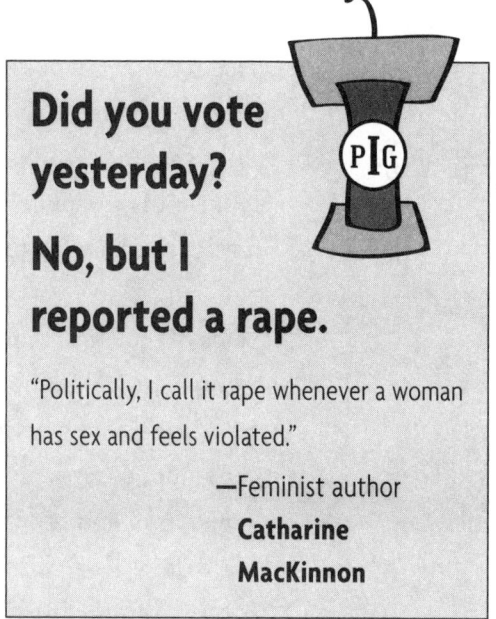

Did you vote yesterday?

No, but I reported a rape.

"Politically, I call it rape whenever a woman has sex and feels violated."

—Feminist author
Catharine MacKinnon

Of course, there are reasons why abuse within marriage may go unreported. Many wives—who may be dependent on their husbands for economic support or who don't want their children to lose a relationship with their father—may hesitate to report violent husbands. As Gallagher and Waite emphasize even a "tiny fraction of fifty-three million married couples in America adds up to hundreds of thousands of injured spouses each year." Yet given that these incidents occur in just a fraction of all marriages, it seems reasonable to assume that marriage itself is not the cause of this violence.[17]

The fact that marriage may reduce the likelihood of violence[18] and the likelihood that women will be victims of a crime are just a few of the lesser known benefits of marriage. As will be discussed in the next chapter, young women often receive a lot of politically incorrect misinformation about marriage and divorce.

The dubious origins of the one-in-four statistic

According to the Department of Justice, more than 150,000 women were the victims of rape or attempted rape in the United States in 2001–02.[19] For many reasons, this number may understate the number of women who experience such an attack. Some women may be reluctant to come forward out of misplaced shame, or because they have a relationship with the attacker that makes it difficult to report his crime. Some may just want to avoid the police and the courts.

Since it is reasonable to assume that this statistic under-estimates the prevalence of rape in the United States, what's a better estimate of its true frequency?

One of the most common statistics used by women's studies centers—and repeated by the media—is that one-in-four college women are victims of rape or attempted rape. It's a shocking ratio; if true it would raise the number of rapes in the United States well above 150,000. Where did it come from and how was it derived?

In *Who Stole Feminism*, Christina Hoff Sommers details the origins of the one-in-four statistic. In 1982, Mary Koss, who had written for *Ms.*

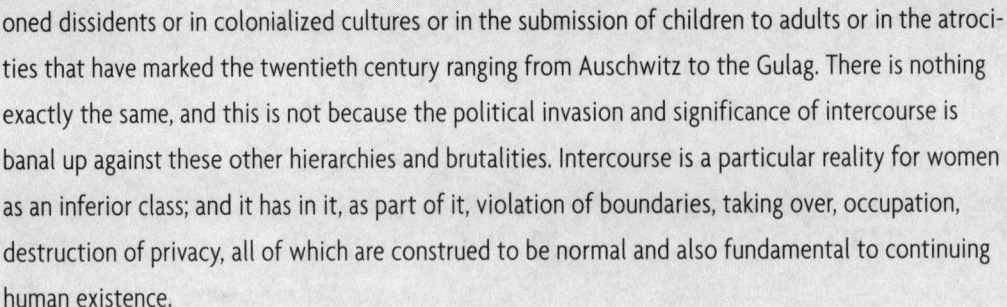

What a Feminist Icon Said:

There is no analogue anywhere among subordinated groups of people to this experience of being made for intercourse: for penetration, entry, occupation. There is no analogue in occupied countries or in dominated races or in imprisoned dissidents or in colonialized cultures or in the submission of children to adults or in the atrocities that have marked the twentieth century ranging from Auschwitz to the Gulag. There is nothing exactly the same, and this is not because the political invasion and significance of intercourse is banal up against these other hierarchies and brutalities. Intercourse is a particular reality for women as an inferior class; and it has in it, as part of it, violation of boundaries, taking over, occupation, destruction of privacy, all of which are construed to be normal and also fundamental to continuing human existence.

Andrea Dworkin, *Intercourse*. http://www.nostatusquo.com/ACLU/dworkin/Intercoursel.html

Magazine, surveyed three thousand college women. Their responses to three questions were used to determine if they had been raped: Have you had sexual intercourse when you didn't want to because a man gave you alcohol or drugs? Have you had sexual intercourse when you didn't want to because a man threatened or used some degree of physical force (twisting your arm, holding you down, etc.) to make you? And, have you had sexual acts (anal or oral intercourse or penetration by objects other than the penis) when you didn't want to because a man threatened to use some degree of physical force (twisting your arm, holding you down, etc.) to make you?

Based on responses to these questions, researchers concluded that 15 percent of women surveyed had been raped and 12 percent had experienced an attempted rape. Therefore, a total of more than 27 percent of women were either the victim of rape or attempted rape.[20] This is the origin of the one-in-four statistic.

There's important information that's not reflected in that number. For example, only 25 percent of the women who Koss counted as having been raped described the incident as rape themselves. Nearly half described the incident as "miscommunication" and 11 percent said that they didn't feel victimized.

Sommers describes how scholars questioned the accuracy of the figure. A professor at Berkeley's School of Social Welfare noted the problems associated with the question, "have you had sexual intercourse when you didn't want to because a man gave you alcohol or drugs." Anyone who drank too much and had a sexual encounter might answer yes even though the regrettable incident probably wasn't rape:

> If your date mixes a pitcher of margaritas and encourages you
> to drink with him and you accept a drink, have you been
> "administered" an intoxicant, and has your judgment been
> impaired? Certainly, if you passout and are molested, one

would call it rape. But if you drink and, while intoxicated, engage in sex that you later come to regret, have you been raped? Koss does not address these questions specifically, she merely counts your date as a rapist and you as a rape statistic if you drank with your date and regret having sex with him.[21]

Koss also found that four in ten of the women she counted as victims of rape, and one out of three victims of attempted rape, went on to have intercourse with their so-called attacker again. While Koss ponders potential reasons these women would return to their attackers, Sommers offers a more simple explanation:

> Since most of those Koss counts as rape victims did not regard themselves as having been raped, why not take this fact and the fact that so many went back to their partners as reasonable indications that they had not been raped to begin with?[22]

Reporters who had examined this study estimated that if you eliminate women who didn't think that they had been raped and those who had responded affirmatively to the alcohol and drug question, instead of one in four women being victims of rape or attempted rape, between one in twenty-two and one in thirty-three are victims, or between 3 to 5 percent of women. This lower estimate is still alarming and probably understates the exact number—women may be reluctant even to admit having been raped in an anonymous survey.

A Book You're Not Supposed to Read

Ceasefire! Why Women and Men Must Join Forces to Achieve True Equality, Cathy Young; New York, The Free Press, 1999.

Another study of four thousand women, compiled in the report "Rape in America" found that one in eight American women—or about 12 percent—had been the victim of forcible rape, which was defined as "an event that occurred without the woman's consent, involved the use of force or threat of force, and involved sexual penetration of the victim's vagina, mouth, or rectum." More than eight in ten did not report the crime to the police.

Yet with all the problem regarding underreporting, these lower numbers are a significant improvement over a figure which is plainly too high, and inevitably leads to an hysterical fear that one quarter of *all* American women—some forty million—will be raped.

More research is needed to get a better understanding of the prevalence of rape in our country, even if knowing the exact number is impossible. Greater efforts need to be made to reduce the number of women (and men) who are victims of this brutal crime. But given that the one-in-four statistic is almost certainly inflated, it should not to be taught as gospel— if for no other reason than it may alarm young women unnecessarily.

Defining rape

Part of the uncertainty about the prevalence of rape may stem from the increased ambiguity about the definition of the crime. While a dictionary provides a seemingly straightforward definition of "forcing another person to submit to sex acts, especially sexual intercourse," what constitutes "force" has become murky. In particular, in situations involving alcohol, it's sometimes difficult to distinguish what's rape and what's simply poorly thought out sex.

Many feminists have pushed for a very broad definition of rape. Feminist Catharine MacKinnon's definition of rape—"politically, I call it rape whenever a woman has sex and feels violated"—is tremendously open-ended, suggesting that there's essentially no time that a man can feel confident that a woman could not later decide to characterize their sexual interlude as rape.

In *Ceasefire! Why Women and Men Must Join Forces to Achieve True Equality*, Cathy Young catalogues how this ambiguity has created significant problems in the legal system. A liberal definition of rape has opened the door for women who, for example, drink too much and then have sex to accuse their partner later of having raped them. Women who initially say no, but then continue to engage in sexual activity leading to intercourse, have accused men of rape even though they faced no physical threats and did not refuse again, which was sadly construed by their partners as having constituted a change of mind. This new standard for what constitutes rape has led to the incarceration of innocent men accused of a brutal crime by women motivated by spite or jealousy.

As Young details, the desire to give the accusing woman the benefit of the doubt stems from an understandable impulse to correct the historical mistreatment of rape victims, who were often made to feel as though they

It's a woman's prerogative to change her mind.

Date rape is unwanted sexual activity that can be distinguished from ordinary rape by the absence of overt violence. If a woman's date violently attacks her and literally forces her to have sex, then what we have is rape without adjectives, not "date" rape. In some cases of date rape, a female college student claims she was raped by her date, while the male insists that the sexual act was consensual. Sometimes, alcohol consumption has clouded the picture of who did what, said what, and meant what. She didn't say no clearly enough; she wasn't clear in her own mind what she wanted. Or maybe she was clear in her own mind that she didn't want it, but she allowed herself to be talked into it and then regretted it later. That process of "talking her into it" becomes the act of aggression that justifies the description of the act as a rape.

Jennifer Roback Morse, *Smart Sex: Finding Life-Long Love in a Hook-Up World* were responsible for causing the crime. However, it's unavoidable that rape—particularly date rape or rape that occurs between acquaintances who have engaged in some sexual contact—often comes down to a situation of "he-said, she-said." While it's important to take the woman's accusations very seriously, it's also important not to lose sight of the rights of the accused. Innocent until proven guilty is an important tenant of our legal system and must not be thrown out simply because of sympathy for the victim.

Women also should consider the social implications of such an expansive definition of rape. By implying that it may be rape anytime a woman has intercourse after consuming alcohol, feminists are suggesting that women are incapable of making decisions when drinking—hardly consistent with the idea of women as capable, independent, and equal.

The notion that once "no" has been uttered, anything after that is rape constitutes a loss of liberty for women. While many colleges and universities have attempted to impose guidelines and speech codes for how to obtain consent during a sexual encounter, such rules ignore how human beings tend to act. Most women (and men) are more coy in sexual situations, and don't want to engage in a lengthy, technical discussion about precisely which intimate acts may occur. One study revealed that six in ten sexually active college women had actually said "no" to sex, even when they intended ultimately to engage in intercourse and nearly all had said "no" when they were still making up their minds.

Conclusion

Violence against women is a problem in the United States. Women need to be prepared to protect themselves and take precautions to minimize their risk of attack. Young women should be particularly aware of the potential for violence and know that even seemingly nice guys can turn out to be bad. But they should recognize that such men are outliers, violence isn't inevitable, and that such crimes are an aberration in American society.

Chapter Seven

MARRIAGE: HAPPIER EVER AFTER

*M*any people think marriage is in trouble. It's common knowledge that divorce rates soared during the second half of the twentieth century while rates of marriage declined. An increasing number of couples are also choosing to forgo or at least postpone marriage and cohabitate, believing that under this arrangement they can enjoy many of the benefits of marriage without the commitment and responsibilities.

Many factors contributed to marriage's decline, including changes in divorce laws, the sexual revolution, and women's increased economic independence. Feminists' assault on marriage also has played a role in devaluing marriage. Radical feminists view marriage as a cruel trap for women, perpetuating patriarchy, and keeping women subservient to men. They lament the roles that women and men tend to assume in traditional marriages, believing that women get the worse deal from the marriage contract.

In spite of this negative perception of marriage and the high rate of divorce, most young women still aspire to marry. These women should be assured that marriage is a reasonable goal, associated with greater health, happiness, and financial security.

Guess what?

- Radical feminists view marriage as a cruel trap for women, perpetuating patriarchy, and keeping women subservient to men.

- It's important for young women to recognize that cohabitation and marriage are not equivalent.

- Married women report higher levels of sexual activity and satisfaction than their single counterparts.

Feminists' rocky relationship with marriage

The feminist movement has a long history of viewing marriage with suspicion, and some radical feminists have gone so far as to call for women to boycott marriage entirely. A radical organization formed in the 1960s called "The Feminist" included the following restriction on marriage for its membership:

> (a) Because THE FEMINISTS consider the institution of marriage inherently inequitable, both in its formal (legal) and informal (social) aspects, and
>
> (b) Because we consider the institution a primary formalization of the persecution of women, and
>
> (c) Because we consider the rejection of this institution both in theory and in practice a primary mark of the radical feminist,
>
> WE HAVE A MEMBERSHIP QUOTA: THAT NO MORE THAN ONE-THIRD OF OUR MEMBERSHIP CAN BE PARTICIPANTS IN EITHER A FORMAL (WITH LEGAL CONTRACT) OR INFORMAL (E.G., LIVING WITH A MAN) INSTANCE OF THE INSTITUTION OF MARRIAGE.[1]

Even members of the more mainstream feminist movement, such as Robin Morgan, who became the editor of *Ms. Magazine*, wanted to end marriage as we know it: "We can't destroy the inequities between men and women until we destroy marriage."[2]

Eventually, some feminists came to recognize the problems associated with this hostility to an institution that many women value. In 1981, Betty Friedan (who many argue launched the modern feminist movement) urged the feminist movement to consider the positive role that marriage and family play in many women's lives and to move beyond its reflexive hostility:

The women's movement is being blamed, above all, for the destruction of the family. Churchman and sociologists proclaim that the American family, as it has always been defined, is becoming an "endangered species," with the rising divorce rate and the enormous increase in single-parent families and people—especially women—living alone. Women's advocation of their age-old responsibilities for the family is also being blamed for the apathy and moral delinquency of the "me generation."

I think we must at least admit and begin openly to discuss feminist denial of the importance of family, of women's own needs to give and get love and nurture, tender loving care.[3]

Even as the mainstream feminist movement attempts to moderate its stance on marriage, women's studies textbooks still present a negative view of marriage. They warn of the dangers to a women's psyche and encourage women to question whether their desire for marriage is a result of a misogynistic patriarchy rather than a true reflection of their preferences. A chapter entitled "Women's Personal Lives: The Effects of Sexism on Self and Relationships," in one introductory textbook includes subheadings such as: "The Case against Traditional Marriage" and "The Feminine Role in Traditional Marriage: A Setup."

The textbook avoids condemning the institution of marriage outright—"It is not that feminism is in principle incompatible with

> ## She's married. Not that there's anything wrong with that.
>
> We must stop repeating the absurd mantra "it's okay to be single," and adopt the more aggressive stance that, "it's not okay to be married."
>
> **—Jaclyn Geller,** *Here Comes the Bride: Women, Weddings, and the Marriage Mystique*

marriage. (Although some feminist believe that it is, others do not, and many feminists marry.)"[4]—and claims simply to take a "more objective glance" at marriage. In truth, marriage is portrayed as an institution designed to benefit men and imprison women. Consider the following passage:

> The fantasy—the marriage myth, a mystical tale of love, romance, and marriage—for women who marry, for women who do not, and for those who unmarry, exercises incredible power over how we live our lives. Even though the very smallest minority of families fits the fairy-tale version—Mama at home, Papa at work—and even though the very smallest minority of couples live the happily-ever-after-forever romance, the myth functions. It undergirds our expectations and colors our relationships. The marriage myth operates on our consciousness even when it is completely absent from reality, even though the story is utterly false.[5]

Utterly false? If there are really young women under the delusion that marriage guarantees life-long bliss, then certainly they should be advised that all relationships, including marriage, will include compromises and some difficult times. However, to call the image of a happy marriage "utterly false" reveals hostility to the institution that's out of step with the average married woman.

Women's textbooks trumpet research suggesting that married women are the most depressed and least happy members of our society. Feminists lament how women typically take on duties such as childcare and housework, even when they work outside the home, while men are expected to do nothing but focus on their careers. Basically, they argue that women get a bad bargain from marriage and should think about renegotiating their contracts.[6]

New York University professor Jaclyn Geller's book, *Here Comes the Bride: Women, Weddings, and the Marriage Mystique* attempts to convince the reader not only that our culture has placed too high a value on romance and getting married, but that marriage is an evil institution that ought to be shunned by women. She dissects the accoutrements surrounding courtship and the "wedding industry," highlighting how our society has set up a system of rewards for those who enter matrimony, excluding those who are single.

She argues that the fixation on this one romantic relationship as the pinnacle of existence crowds out a healthy appreciation for the importance of other intimate relationships, such as friendships and family. Single girls, even in an age when their lives are often depicted as exciting and glamorous, are encouraged to think of their lives as beginning only after they have found a marriage partner. Geller laments the use of the word "single" itself, which fails to acknowledge the myriad relationships enjoyed by unmarried women, implying that there is something missing or that she is "alone."

Certainly, it's important for women and society at large to recognize that getting married isn't right for everybody and that meaningful lives exist outside of matrimony. The caricatured "spinster" hardly represents the dynamic lives led by many single women. But instead of encouraging greater respect for the choices made by women including the decision not to marry, Geller attempts to corral society into condemning marriage and those who choose to marry—even feminist icons. She considers Gloria Steinem's decision to marry as a betrayal, adding:

> I would argue that choosing to uphold an institution rooted in the barter of women as property, an institution that devalues friendship and envisions female existence in terms of a romantic narrative of male redemption, is not valid, not right at any age.[7]

This hostility to marriage simply ignores its many benefits and the important function it provides to society.

Popular culture: celebrating weddings, not marriage

While feminist instructors may warn young women away from the altar, many other messages young women receive outside the classroom continue to foster the desire to get married. Glenn and Marquardt's study of college women found that more than eight in ten of those surveyed still thought "being married" was an important goal and more than six in ten hoped to meet their future spouse during college.

Women are reminded of the desirability of getting married—and weddings in particular—with every trip down the grocery store aisle. Women's magazines regularly describe how to get your significant other to pop the question and entire magazines are dedicated to planning the perfect wedding, honeymoon, and bridal showers. It's no wonder that the bridal industry is a $35 billion business annually in the United States.[8]

Comparatively little ink is given to the meaning of marriage after the wedding cake top is put in the freezer (unless it's about improving your sex life). In popular culture, weddings are typically the ending, and the happy ending, of a television series or a movie.

This decade has seen a rash of reality television shows from *Who Wants to Marry a Millionaire* and *The Bachelor* that use marriage as a prize in sort of game show. *Friends* concluded with a string of marriages, but these seemingly serious events were overshadowed by the sitcoms

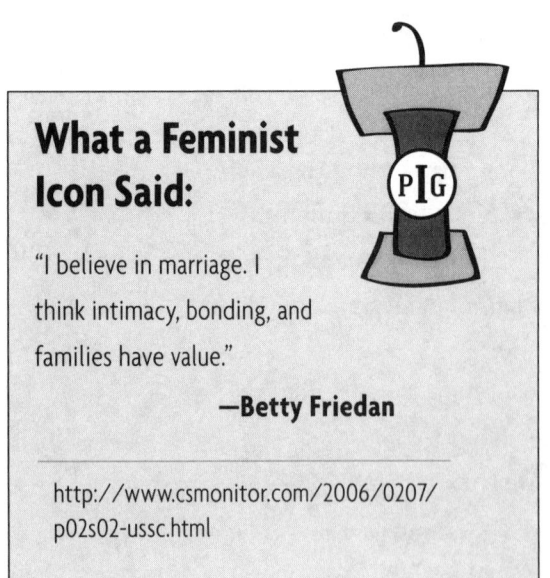

What a Feminist Icon Said:

"I believe in marriage. I think intimacy, bonding, and families have value."

—Betty Friedan

http://www.csmonitor.com/2006/0207/p02s02-ussc.html

casual treatment of marriage, from Ross's series of divorces, Phoebe's green card–seeking husband, to Ross and Rachel's short-lived Vegas wedding.

Real-life marriage is more than a wedding. Marriage is a lifetime commitment that requires long-term perspective. This is particularly true given the increased prevalence of divorce in American culture. Fewer and fewer young women and men are growing up in households that provide the best role model for how marriage is supposed to work in real life: married parents.

It's particularly important for young women from broken homes to hear the facts about the positive side of marriage. Everyone knows that nearly half of marriages fail. But that cup-half-empty statistic also means that more than half of marriages (and well more than half of first marriages) succeed. Young women need to know that achieving life-long companionship with a spouse is possible and that marriage has many important benefits in terms of your health, financial security, and long-term happiness.

Marriage: happier ever after

Waite and Gallagher, in *The Case for Marriage*, have catalogued research on the effects of marriage on both men and women. They conclude that both genders exhibit better mental health and are happier when married than when single, cohabitating, divorced, separated, or widowed.

Waite and Gallagher highlight several studies that support this finding. One of the most convincing is a longitudinal study that tracks the same individuals over time. The researchers followed up initial interviews after five years, during which time some of the subjects married, others divorced or separated, and some remained single. They found that marriage substantially improved individuals' mental health while divorce and separation were associated with deterioration in mental and emotional well-being. Waite and Gallagher note the importance of this study since it looked at individuals before and after they experienced a change in marital status, and were therefore able to rule out the hypothesis that happier people marry:

> They found the act of getting married actually makes people happier and healthier; conversely, getting a divorce reverses these gains—even when we take into account prior measures of mental and emotional health.[9]

Waite and Gallagher also highlighted data from a survey of fourteen thousand adults, in which married men and women were significantly more likely to report that they were satisfied with life. Forty percent of married individuals said they were very happy compared to less than one-quarter of those single and cohabiting, 15 percent of those separated, and 18 percent of those who were divorced.[10]

Married people also were about half as likely as singles or cohabitators to report general unhappiness with their lives. Those individuals who were divorced were two-and-a-half times more likely to report being "not too happy," and the widowed almost three times more likely.[11]

It's notable that, in all cases, less than a majority of women interviewed report that they are generally "very happy" with their lives. This supports feminist claims that young women should not delude themselves that marriage guarantees bliss or even a consistent state of "happily ever after." But the contention that marriage is the *cause* of unhappiness is not supported by the facts. Evidence suggests that marriage increases the odds of long-term happiness compared to the other paths women can take in their relationships.

The Pew Research Center for the People & the Press surveyed 1,101 American women in 1997 and asked about their attitudes towards marriage. While married women responded overwhelmingly that their marriage was a source of happiness, nearly half also revealed that it was a source of frustration: "Nine out of ten women say their marriage makes them happy all or most of the time. Nearly half find it frustrating at least some of the time."[12]

Feminists would note that it is impossible to isolate "true" happiness since a portion of a married woman's happiness may be attributable to meeting some social norm.

A Book You're Not Supposed to Read

The Case for Marriage: Why Married People Are Happier, Healthier, and Better Off Financially, Linda J. Waite and Maggie Gallagher; New York, Doubleday, 2000.

She has successfully fit in, and thus has avoided the societal condemnation that comes with being a "spinster," "divorcee," or even a widow.[13]

Undoubtedly, social pressures—both positive and negative—play a role in the decision to marry. Young women should be aware of how such pressure affects their decisions and may drive them to enter an unwise marriage. But feminist educators cheat women by ignoring their desire to marry and evidence of their higher levels of happiness. Discounting women's responses or insisting that their desires are actually the result of male manipulation smacks of the kind of sexism that feminists claim to abhor.

Marriage: a good financial plan

Marriage is also good for women's pocketbooks, savings, and long-term financial stability. Couples who stay married are far less likely to slip into poverty than people who never marry.[14] Most of the book, *The Two-Income Trap*, written by Elizabeth Warren and Amelia Warren Tyagi, is dedicated to the financial problems faced by many American families; in particular, dual-earner couples who rely on both salaries to make ends meet. But it also highlights some of the ways that marriage helps ward off financial hardship. A stay-at-home spouse is compared to a "safety net" or an insurance policy.[15] If the other spouse loses a job or gets ill, the stay-at-home spouse can look for outside work in order to make up for any loss of income.

Marriage also helps encourage thrift because spouses who are more responsible about handling money tend to take on a disproportionate share of those tasks.[16] Marriage also appears to encourage savings. Waite and Gallagher highlight a study of people's savings behavior over a five year period and found that the assets of couples who stayed married increased by more than 7 percent per year. These effects could not be explained by improved education, health, or even higher earnings.[17]

Marriage leads to better health

Data suggests that married women are better off in terms of health. The Centers for Disease Control and Prevention conducted a survey of 127,545 adults over age eighteen, and found that those who were married generally were healthier than their non-married counterparts:

> Regardless of population subgroup (age, sex, race, Hispanic origin, education, income, or nativity) or health indictor (fair or poor health, limitations in activities, low back pain, headaches, serious psychological distress, smoking, or leisure-time physical inactivity), married adults were generally found to be healthier than adults in other marital status categories.... The one negative health indicator for which married adults had a higher prevalence was overweight or obesity.[18]

This report found married adults were less likely to suffer from health conditions such as headaches and serious psychological distress, and were less likely to engage in risky behaviors such as smoking, heavy drinking, or physical inactivity.[19]

There are several potential causes for the link between marriage and health. For men—who experience the greatest gains in health from marriage—the reasons seem obvious: Wives nag their husbands to go to the doctor and discourage unhealthy behaviors like heavy drinking and smoking. For women, the increase in wealth may be among the most significant factors in improving their health. But both men and women may enjoy health benefits from marriage simply because a sick spouse may feel as if he or she has something to live for and because of the extra care and support given by the marriage partner.[20]

The sexier side of marriage

A running joke in the popular 1990s sitcom *Married with Children* is Peggy Bundy's constant pestering of her husband, Al Bundy, for sex. Sex with his wife is depicted as the ultimate chore for Al, who would much rather plop down on his couch and watch TV.

It may surprise some to read that—in spite of the dearth of images of sex within the confines of marriage in a culture otherwise saturated in sexual imagery—married women report higher levels of sexual activity and satisfaction than their single counterparts. In a survey of 3,500 adults conducted by Edward Laumann at the University of Chicago, 42 percent of married women said they found sex extremely emotionally and physically satisfying. Just 31 percent of single women who had a sex partner reported the same level of satisfaction.[21]

Shacking up isn't the same as tying the knot

Some young women may think that they don't need marriage to realize these benefits: Cohabitation—or living with your significant other—fills the same purposes as marriage while avoiding the downsides of commitment and the potential for having to legally divorce.

Many more Americans are choosing to cohabitate. In 1970, about 500,000 opposite-sex couples lived together; today, nearly five million couples are doing so. More than half of all couples getting married this year have lived together.[22] Few couples choose to cohabitate indefinitely, most either marry or break up within five years. About half of cohabitating relationships ultimately result in marriage and half end up going their separate ways.

There are many reasons for the surge in couples choosing not to marry—or at least postpone marriage until after they live together. Since premarital sex is no longer taboo in our society, living together has become much more socially acceptable. Many people decide to cohabitate based on financial factors, such as the potential to save on rent and share other expenses. The prevalence of divorce and desire to avoid entering into an unwise marriage may also motivate people to cohabitate in an attempt to better assess if they are compatible over the long term.

Those attempting to head off divorce by first cohabitating may be disappointed to learn that research suggests that cohabitating may increase the odds of divorce. Couples who live together prior to marriage are twice as likely to divorce as those who don't and report more arguing, less satisfaction, and poorer communication.[23]

Nancy Wartik, writing on the cohabitation phenomenon in *Psychology Today*, offers the following explanation:

> Why would something that seems so sensible potentially be so damaging? Probably the reigning explanation is the inertia hypothesis, the idea that many of us slide into marriage without ever making an explicit decision to commit. We move in together, we get comfortable, and pretty soon marriage starts to seem like the path of least resistance. Even if the relationship is only tolerable, the next stage starts to seem inevitable.
>
> Because we have different standards for living partners than for life partners, we may end up married to someone we never would have originally considered for the long haul.[24]

Wartik describes how cohabitation may lead some men and women to wed "more out of guilt or fear than love."

Similarly, Jennifer Roback Morse highlights how cohabitation—by placing two individuals in such an intimate setting where they not only have sex but sleep next to each other each night—helps create an "involuntary chemical commitment." While the original purpose of cohabitation may have been to expose flaws that would make the marriage ill-advised, in reality, it may make the individuals involved less willing to break off the relationship, even if it's flawed, by increasing feelings of attachment.[25]

Cohabitation can drive individuals to make an unwise marriage, but the opposite also can be true. Many young women who move in with a man expect that it will lead to marriage—researchers have found that women are more likely to see moving in as a step toward marriage than are men—but find out that their partner has different expectations.[26] Once they've moved in and invested additional time in the relationship expecting to be proposed to, women become more reluctant to bring up the subject of marriage or ultimately to leave the relationship and face the single dating life. Again, age and its fertility implications contribute to this dynamic and make women move vulnerable and less powerful.

Cohabitating relationships also fail to provide the security of marriage since they are, by their nature, inherently less secure than marriage.

Women's Studies 101: You get an A if you do not marry

Women have to be conned into institutionalized marriage and motherhood.... She has to be taught that without a man at her side she is incomplete, and without marriage and motherhood she can find no lasting fulfillment. Her desires and life chances thus narrowed, a woman is primed not to rebel against domestic inequities. Feminism promotes such a rebellion.

—Mary F. Rogers and C.D. Garrett, *Who's Afraid of Women's Studies: Feminisms in Everyday Life*

Morse uses the metaphor of taking the relationship (or the other person) out for a "test drive."[27] You are expected to try to act exactly as you would if married so that the other party can assess your suitability as a spouse. If you in some way don't measure up to your partner's expectations, you can be returned and there aren't supposed to be any hard feelings. Of course, it's hard to act exactly as you would absent the actual commitment—you may attempt to put on a good performance in order to be judged "marriage material" or to withhold some of yourself so that you'll feel less vulnerable if you are ultimately judged unworthy.

It's become politically correct for society not to differentiate between those couples who are cohabitating and those who are married. Yet it's important for young women to recognize that cohabitation and marriage are not equivalent. Cohabitation doesn't provide the same benefits as marriage and may put women on an unwelcome path toward an unwise marriage, or no marriage at all.

More than just husband and wife

Marriage does more than just benefit those who choose to wed: it also affects society. One reason why marriage is celebrated in cultures around the globe.

The celebration surrounding marriage receives some of the harshest complaints from feminists. Jaclyn Geller's hostility to marriage centers on what she sees as the inflated importance society places on the union, showering those who choose to make this decision with gifts, parties, and attention. No other relationship receives such outward approval and support.

In *The New Single Woman*, E. Kay Trimberger, a professor of women's and gender studies at Sonoma State University, celebrates the lives of single women and encourages society to recognize and validate the choices that women make in choosing to forgo marriage.[28] Unlike Geller, Trimberger isn't hostile to marriage and simply seeks to eradicate the lingering social stigma and stereotypes associated with being a single woman. Trimberger makes many valid points and celebrates the important roles that friendships and families can play in creating a rich life for those who choose not to marry.

But Geller and Trimberger ignore the unique benefits that marriage affords society. Marriage *is* unlike any other relationship: it's a contract that carries a host of legal and social obligations that affect everyone.

Spouses are legally obliged to assume financial responsibility for each other. As discussed previously, Warren and Tyagi highlight how spouses are essentially an insurance policy, in case one loses a job or becomes ill or disabled. This not only benefits those spouses, but the rest of society, which may be compelled to come to the aid of someone who suffers such a loss.

The New Single Woman highlights how single individuals create relationships based on mutual trust and interdependence that share important similarities to marriage. This is certainly true, but those relationships don't compare to the legal and social obligations borne in a marriage. There may be tremendous examples of generosity and commitment between friends, but those relationships are not as dependable as marriage.

Trimberger dedicates a chapter to how communities of friends help each other through illness and even death. Yet she emphasizes the importance of building a larger community of individuals for support since it's "unrealistic" to assume that a best friend is going to be able to meet all of one's needs in such a time of crisis.

This is a striking contrast to marriage. Of course, a spouse won't necessarily be able to fulfill all of his or her partner's needs and will benefit from the love and support of an extend network of family and friends. But it's taken for granted that the spouse is responsible for tending to their sick husband or wife and will shoulder the primary burden. It would be socially unacceptable to do otherwise. A woman who chooses to abandon her husband when he is struck by illness would face significant

A Book You're Not Supposed to Read

Smart Sex: Finding Life-Long Love in a Hook-Up World, Jennifer Roback Morse; Dallas, Spence Publishing Company, 2005.

social pressure from disapproving friends and family. There are times when spouses fail each other, but for the most part the vow of "in sickness and in health" is taken seriously. Society enforces this expectation not just for moral reasons, but because it helps preserve order and reduces the burden on everyone.

Society also has an interest in upholding the importance of marriage because of marriage's unique role in nurturing the next generation. The evidence is overwhelming that children raised within a stable marriage are less likely to commit crimes, abuse drugs and alcohol, have out of wedlock births, and drop out of school than peers raised outside of marriage. In short, children from married couples are far less likely to end up as drains on society and are more likely to be productive citizens. It's in all of our interest to encourage stable marriages to increase our society's long-term welfare.

This doesn't mean that those who are single should be stigmatized, but it does help explain why marriage holds a special place in our culture. It isn't simply that we love a wedding and want to celebrate an occasion that promises to bring two individuals happiness: it's in our collective interest to perpetuate a culture that values healthy marriages.

Conclusion

Marriage isn't for everyone. Single women can and do lead fulfilling lives. But young women who seek a stable marriage should know that their impulse is not simply a result of an oppressive society—it's a natural goal consistent with long-term happiness, financial security, and good health.

Chapter Eight

DIVORCE

Most of popular culture acknowledges the desirability of *getting* married, but says little about the importance of *staying* married. It's now commonly accepted that a marriage should be maintained only for so long as the couple finds that it brings them happiness. Divorce is seen as the appropriate ending to marriages that aren't bringing personal fulfillment.

Divorce is sometimes unavoidable. It's a step, however, that shouldn't be taken lightly. Young women contemplating marriage may see divorce as the equivalent of a "do-over"—an easy way to reverse the decision to marry if the relationship doesn't turn out as they had hoped. But divorce isn't a do-over. It's no guarantee of future happiness, and many women find that they trade one set of problems for another.

And while it is no longer politically correct to encourage a couple to consider how divorce may affect their children, parents weighing whether to end their marriage should be aware of divorce's potential long-term impact. Research suggests that children whose parents divorce face immediate problems due to their parents' break up, and continue to suffer the effects of the divorce throughout their lives.

Guess what?

- Many women experience regret after divorce and wish they had given their marriages another chance.

- Divorce is a big gamble for women seeking long-term happiness.

- Surveys regularly show that children of divorce are more likely to suffer from pathologies and exhibit antisocial behaviors.

Society's changing attitudes toward divorce

Society has increasingly accepted divorce, even when it involves families with children. In 1962, just half of women disagreed with the statement "when there are children in the family, parents should stay together even if they don't get along." Fifteen years later, more than eight in ten mothers surveyed disagreed with this statement—in other words, fewer than two in ten thought that a couple should stay together for the sake of the children.

Divorce has become a regular, unremarkable event in popular culture. From Brittany Spears' twenty-four-hour Vegas marriage to the carefully chronicled saga of Brad Pitt and Jennifer Aniston's breakup, tabloids and entertainment magazines cover like a sport celebrity marriages, the divorces that quickly follow, and the next relationships that often begin before the first ends. Divorce is common in movies and television; often, these media showcase divorce's dramatic affects on family members, but rarely is the decision to split questioned.

The movie *Stepmom*, for example, focuses on the tumultuous aftermath of divorce. The father Luke (played by Jack Harris) struggles to bring his new love, the significantly younger Isabel (played by Julia Roberts), into his children's lives, while his ex-wife, Jackie, (played by Susan Sarandon) finds out that she's terminally ill with cancer.

Stepmom explores the changing relationship between the two women, as well as the difficult adjustment the children face as they cope with a new family member entering their lives as their mother exits. The children express great frustration at their helplessness—their parents' divorce and father's remarriage occurred without their consultation. But the adults watching are expected to understand that this marriage was doomed, divorce was necessary, and the kids will be ultimately better off because their parents ended an unhappy marriage.

It isn't just Hollywood movies or flighty superstars that make divorce seem the natural end for marriages that aren't blissful. Even prominent

Christian vocalist Amy Grant, who divorced her husband of sixteen years, received advice from a counselor that marriage should be maintained only so long as both partners are happy. In an interview conducted by *ChristianityToday*, Grant explained:

> [God] didn't create this institution [of marriage] so He could just plug people into it. He provided this so that people could enjoy each other to the fullest." Grant herself adds: "If you have two people that are not thriving healthily in a situation, I say remove the marriage. Let them heal.[1]

Clearly, divorce—once seen as taboo and an absolute last resort for the truly miserable married couple—has become commonly accepted as the appropriate outcome for imperfect marriages.

Facilitating divorce; changing marriage

Not only has the stigma associated with divorce been lessened if not entirely eliminated, but laws have changed to facilitate divorce. During the 1970s and 1980s, all fifty states adopted "no fault" divorce laws that gave couples the ability to file for divorce without claiming that the other spouse had in some way "broken" the marriage contract by committing adultery, a felony, or being abusive.

As divorce became easier, it became more common. Since 1960, the number of divorces has skyrocketed—more than doubling over fifteen years. The divorce rate peaked in 1980 and has slightly declined in the last twenty years.[2]

Changes in the divorce law aren't entirely responsible for the rise in the numbers of divorces; numerous other factors—from the sexual revolution to the increase in women's employment and financial independence—also played a role in making divorce more prevalent. However,

At the Movies

"You never asked me if I wanted a new mother. You never even asked me if I liked her!"

—Anna Harrison,
Stepmom

certainly these changes in law helped make divorce a more convenient option for many married couples.

This growing availability and acceptance of divorce undeniably has had some positive results. It gave some women and men in truly unhappy or abusive relationships greater opportunity to exit the situation and a new chance to seek love and happiness. However, the divorce revolution also has imposed extensive costs on society and families.

At its core, marriage is a contract. This contract's importance becomes clear when couples reach a courtroom seeking divorce; but it also affects how couples behave during and before they enter into their marriage. In a marriage, individuals make substantial investments in each other. They intertwine finances, and both partners make decisions in the interest of the marriage, not merely for themselves. This is particularly true for women who make substantial personal sacrifices, such as forgoing a career to care for children, to benefit the couple with the understanding that their husbands will provide financial support over the long-term.

Even some women's studies textbooks admit that the increased ease of divorce has been a mixed-blessing for women. The following reveals a bias that assumes that the woman is the innocent party, but the logic holds true for a wronged wife or husband:

> Although this change has made divorces easier to obtain, these procedures have pitfalls. Consider the homemaker who has been victim of cruelty or who finds out that her husband has been having affairs. In earlier days, she could have charged her husband with the fault and then sought a divorce. As the inno-cent party, she would probably have been awarded a consider-

able portion of the couple's property. Under the current system, if that same woman and her husband divorce on no-fault grounds, there is no reason for the court to award her any more than her basic share.[3]

Government may have created a new, easier way to dissolve a marriage through no fault divorce, but in the process it eliminated an option: People no longer could enter into a marriage contract that limited the ways that the union could be dissolved.

Some states are attempting to address this problem by offering alternative marriage contracts. In 1997, Louisiana passed the covenant marriage law which gave couples the option of entering into a marriage contract that has more restrictions on how the contract can be dissolved. Several other states have followed suit.

Before considering how public policy might reduce the number of divorces, we must determine whether divorce is really a problem. If the increased ease of divorce means that people are finding greater happiness, then the rise in divorce may not be of concern. If children whose parents divorce really are no worse off, then society need not be concerned about their fates and should assume that happier parents equal happier children.

Yet as the rest of this chapter reveals, research evaluating the impact of divorce on former spouses and their children suggests that there *is* reason to be concerned that divorce harms many adults and their children.

Does divorce improve a woman's chance for happiness?

The politically correct view of divorce is that once women get through the initial turmoil of a heart wrenching break up, they'll be better off having rid themselves of the unhappy relationship. It's commonly known that women often face serious financial hardship after a divorce, but there's an expectation that women's personal lives usually improve after the break up.

Cutting Loose: Why Women Who End Their Marriages Do So Well showcases how divorce benefits women. The author, Ashton Appleton, interviewed fifty women who had initiated their divorces. She states upfront that the women interviewed were self-selected, responding to advertisements or through word-of-mouth, and therefore were in no way statistically representative of the female divorced population as a whole. However, she uses their stories to construct the case that women who divorce tend to be empowered by the experience, leaving them with happier, more fulfilling lives.

Appleton's view of traditional marriage is bleak: "These women came to realize that traditional marriage serves the husband, the wife serves the marriage—and that independence beats servitude."[4] She describes the toll that marriage takes on many women's sense of self: "Marriage reduces many women, who willingly, often unthinkingly, embrace a peculiarly circumscribed identity and set of priorities when they give up being single."[5]

The book does describe some of the difficulties women face during divorce; from the challenge of navigating the legal terrain to the many worries, including a fear of losing control of their children, new financial problems, and insecurities about finding new loves and relationships. But ultimately, Appleton emphasizes the many rewards that women receive after breaking free of a troubled marriage, the pride of taking back their lives, independence, and happiness:

From *Friends*

Ross: First divorce: wife's hidden sexuality, not my fault. Second divorce: said the wrong name at the altar, kind of my fault. Third divorce: they shouldn't let you get married when you're that drunk and have stuff drawn all over your face, Nevada's fault.

The end of a marriage is a loss, but not a failure. On the contrary it is a victory—over inertia, terror, conformity, insecurity, and countless other demons. Every woman who speaks in these pages has suffered enormously. Many wish they had left their marriages sooner, but had to wait until they had marshaled the financial or emotional resources. They are proud of themselves for having gone through with it, and not one regrets it.[6]

Is the experience of Applewhite's subjects emblematic of the experience of most women?

The truth is divorce is a big gamble for women seeking long-term happiness. One group of researchers assessed data from the National Survey of Families and Households (a national representative survey) to evaluate if divorce was generally associated with an increase in happiness. They focused on spouses who had rated their marriages "unhappy" in an initial interview and were re-interviewed five years later. During that time, some had divorced, some had separated and some had remained married.[7] The researchers concluded that: "Unhappily married adults who divorced or separated were no happier, on average, than unhappily married adults who stayed married. Even unhappy spouses who had divorced and remarried were no happier, on average, than unhappy spouses who stayed married."[8]

Like life itself, marriages tend to swing between happiness and unhappiness. Many marriages that had been unhappy during the initial national survey had improved dramatically five years later; while many couples in stable, happy marriages either had divorced or become unhappy during the intervening years. In fact, nearly three out of four divorces that occurred between the interviews happened to adults who had reported being happily married five years earlier. Many of the unhappy marriages had seen just as dramatic turnarounds: The researchers estimate that two out of three unhappily married adults who avoided divorce or separation reported being happily married during the five years follow up interview.[9]

Similarly, Linda Waite and Maggie Gallagher report in *The Case for Marriage* that 86 percent of married people who said they were unhappy in their marriage, but who stayed together, reported higher levels of marital happiness five years later. Some of the worst marriages showed the most dramatic turnarounds, leading the authors to conclude: "Permanent marital unhappiness is surprisingly rare among the couples who stick it out."[10]

How did these unhappy couples turn their marriages around? Researchers set out to answer that question and conducted focus group interviews with fifty-five formerly unhappy husbands and wives whose relationships had dramatically improved. They found that many of the currently happily married spouses had endured periods of significant problems—infidelity, verbal abuse, emotional neglect, and alcoholism—but that these couples had simply outlasted those problems. The couples explained that with time "many of the sources of conflict and distress ease."[11]

None of these researchers condemns divorce or fails to acknowledge the very poor state of many marriages. However, they caution that with divorce, individuals are often trading one set of causes for unhappiness with another set of equally serious problems. Those who divorce have to face many new challenges, including the response of their spouse and children to the divorce, potential custody battles, worries about child support and complying with visitation orders, new financial stresses, a potential move, and creating and maintaining new adult relationships.[12]

Contrary to what Applewhite's interviews suggest, many women do experience regret after divorce and wish they had given their marriages another chance. One survey of those who had divorced in New Jersey found that nearly half wished they and their spouse had tried harder to work through their difference. Four in ten divorced people in Minnesota said they had at least some regrets about their divorce and two in three wished they and their spouses had tried harder to work through their differences.[13]

One of the great hopes of many of those who divorce is that they will go on to find a new, committed relationship that will be more satisfying. In fact, most divorcees do go on to marry again. The rates of remarriage vary by age: about three quarters of women in their twenties who divorce will remarry; a little over half of those in their thirties will remarry; less than a third of those in their forties and just over one in ten of those over fifty. Age doesn't have the same impact on men's remarriage rates; men in their low forties are twice as likely to remarry as are women that age.[14]

While these numbers fit the general perception that there are fewer men available for older divorced woman to marry, there are many potential explanations beyond the availability of partners. Women beyond child bearing age or who have already had children may be less interested in marriage than younger divorcees who are still hoping to build a family. Older divorcees may be more financially stable and so may not be seeking a partner who can help provide financial stability.

A Book You're Not Supposed to Read

The Case against Divorce, Diane Medved, PhD; New York, Ivy Books, 1989.

If rates of remarriage suggest that finding true love after divorce is common, the rates of divorce for second marriages shatter that fantasy. Roughly a quarter of all second marriages end within five years and between 60 to 85 percent of remarriages end within ten years.[15] Even Applewhite, who is relatively bullish on single life, admits that most women find it a mixed bag. She begins by describing single life as "exhilarating" and says that many women thrive in the freedom.[16] Yet she ultimately acknowledges that many divorced women are lonely and long for a male companion.

Many women and men who exit unhappy marriage do go on to find love and happiness in their new lives. But so will many married couples who forgo divorce and instead stick out the rocky times. Women contemplating divorce should do so with their eyes wide open, aware that there are risks to leaving an unhappy marriage, just as there are risks to staying in one.

The kids are all right

Spouses who decide to divorce aren't the only ones affected by the dissolution of their marriage. Divorce also has a profound impact on the children of that marriage.

There often is a disconnect in discussions about the effects of divorce on children. One poll found that nearly two in three Americans agreed that divorce "almost always or frequently harms children," but the same poll found that just one in three thought that parents should stay together and not get a divorce if the marriage isn't working.[17]

Most of the time, we take very seriously research that suggests a certain behavior could adversely affect kids. Even before a baby is born, prospective mothers are pouring over books and magazines on how best to increase her child's future health and happiness, from avoiding a long list of foods—including sushi, tuna fish, soft cheeses, and caffeine—to sleeping on her left side and playing classical music to her growing belly. The chances of complications being caused by a cup of regular coffee or blue cheese dressing may be miniscule, but many mothers want to err on the side of safety.

When it comes to divorce, however, society is more willing to sacrifice kids' interests for the sake of parents. One explanation for why individuals may discount the experience of children in divorce is the ambiguity of the word "harm." If the harm children experience is akin to getting a tetanus shot—a temporary pain that quickly recedes from memory while the protection it affords last for years—then it's altogether appropriate to discount that harm. But if the harm is severe, long-lasting, and with effects that resonate for years, many parents may seriously consider maintaining a less than happy marriage in order to spare children that experience.

In many discussions about divorce, the underlying assumption is that children may have short term problems, but if the parents are happier after the breakup, then ultimately the children will also be happier. This is Applewhite's take on how to put children's experience with divorce in perspective. The women she interviewed, while recognizing the immediate pain experienced by the children, felt that, if anything, the children's long-term prospects were bolstered by divorce.

> Though full of remorse for the suffering it caused their families, especially in the immediate aftermath of the divorce, with only one exception the mothers interviewed for this book do not feel that the experience ultimately harmed their children. In fact, the majority feel their children actually benefited from the change, in ways both predictable and unexpected. Their experiences reflect what studies—including a twenty-year survey of twenty thousand families—have shown but what nevertheless is still not common knowledge: that divorce need not damage children.[18]

Applewhite goes farther to describe her own children's experience with her divorce, noting that "though their grief is real and ongoing, my children are better off because their father and I are no longer together."[19]

Divorce's *kid*-lateral damage

While Applewhite may be correct that research shows that divorce *need not* damage children, the weight of the evidence suggests that most divorces in fact *do* leave a lasting negative impact.

Surveys regularly show that children of divorce are more likely to suffer from pathologies and exhibit antisocial behaviors. Adolescents in divorced families are more likely than peers from intact families to be depressed, get expelled from school, have to repeat a grade, be involved in behavioral problems such as stealing, vandalism, or truancy, use marijuana, cocaine, and cigarettes, and become sexually active.[20] Children raised in stepfamilies are three times more likely to be incarcerated as adults than are those from intact married families.[21]

Some of the most interesting evidence on the long-term effects of divorce comes from Judith Wallerstein, who, along with Julia Lewis and Sandra Blakeslee, wrote the book *The Unexpected Legacy of Divorce: The 25 Year Landmark Study*. Wallerstein began studying a group of 131 children and families who were going through divorce in 1971. She continued to reevaluate them eighteen-months, five, ten, fifteen, and finally twenty-five years later. In the last interview, she was able to locate close to 80 percent of her subjects, now adults. She also interviewed a "control group" of children from intact families with similar backgrounds to her original subjects, whose family life ranged from "harmonious to wretched."[22]

Wallerstein's research shatters what she calls the "cherished myths" about divorce—that happier parents necessarily lead to happier kids and that the trauma kids experienced at the time of divorce is temporary. Her work indicates that many children suffer after a divorce even if their parents are better off and that the effects of divorce continue to materialize years and even decades after the break up. She points to national studies that support her observations, and finds that children of divorce are more likely to exhibit a host of pathologies, from depression and learning disabilities to earlier sexual activity and more unplanned pregnancy, than their peers.

This aggregate data needs to be viewed with caution. It's no surprise that children are better off in a stable, loving home than in a violent marriage that ends in divorce. For a woman in a troubled marriage contemplating divorce, the option of a stable, loving home isn't available. She's already in a troubled marriage, and if she has come to the point of contemplating divorce, she isn't optimistic that the marriage will improve. She has two options: stay in the troubled marriage or divorce. The information she needs is how her children will fair under these two scenarios.

Wallerstein attempts to answer that question and to address bias in the data by comparing children with similar backgrounds. She interviewed control groups of children from intact families, some of whom were as violent and dysfunctional as any divorcing family she encountered, and others in which the parents were moderately unhappy throughout their marriage but choose to stay together. By comparing the children of divorce to these children who had similar upbringings and even similar family lives, she was better able to isolate how divorce itself affected the children:

> One in four of the children in this study started using drugs and alcohol before their fourteenth birthdays. By the time they were seventeen years old, over half of the teenagers were drinking or taking drugs. This number compares with almost 40 percent of all teenagers nationwide....
>
> Early sex was very common among girls in the divorced families.... In our study, one in five had her first sexual experience before the age of fourteen. Over half were sexually active with multiple partners during their high school years. In the comparison group, the great majority of girls postponed sex until the last year of high school or their early years in college. Those who engaged in sexual activity did so as part of an ongoing relationship that lasted an average of a year.[23]

Wallerstein describes the many roles that children take on post-divorce, from acting as a caretaker to younger siblings or a grieving parent to adopting behaviors associated with the absent parent. She highlights how divorce reduces the amount of time that the child typically spends with the parent no longer living in the same residence, and at the same time often results in less access to their primary care-giving parent who is taking on new responsibilities and attempting to rebuild a life of her (or his) own.

Wallerstein cautions those contemplating divorce to recognize that it will not eliminate the problems that previously haunted the couple. Presumably both parents will continue to be involved in raising their children, and they'll interact and have a relationship post-divorce. This often means that problems prevalent during the marriage remain a significant factor in the relationship after the marriage is dissolved. Wallerstein highlights the case of one youngster with a father emotionally abusive to his sister and mother, but who continued that abuse in his post-divorce relationship with his children. Wallerstein concludes: "Larry's experiences reveal that divorce is not the quick solution to a bad marriage that many people understand it to be. High-conflict marriages often lead to high-conflict families after divorce."[24]

A Book You're Not Supposed to Read

The Unexpected Legacy of Divorce: The 25 Year Landmark Study, by Judith S. Wallerstein, Julia M. Lewis, and Sandra Blakeslee; New York, Hyperion, 2000.

Wallerstein's interviews with the children revealed that while often aware that their parents aren't entirely happy or at times fight they valued having the family intact. Even children whose parents were clearly in unhappy marriages were often shocked at the time of divorce and continued afterwards to long for their parents to get back together:

> When one looks at the thousands of children that my colleagues and I have interviewed at our center since 1980, most of whom were from moderately unhappy marriages that ended

in divorce, one message is clear: the children do not say they are happier. Rather, they say flatly, "The day my parents divorced is the day my childhood ended."[25]

Perhaps the most interestingly aspect of Wallerstein's research is her finding that the problems of divorce during childhood are not the end of the trail, but a prelude to what children will face as adults, when Wallerstein sees the most severe impact.[26] She describes the effect of divorce on children as a "cumulative experience" that affects each developmental stage, but most profoundly, when children grow up and seek to create loving, lasting relationships of their own: "Their lack of inner images of a man and a woman in a stable relationship and their memories of their parents' failure to sustain the marriage badly hobbles their search, leading them to heartbreak and even despair."[27]

It's not that children of divorce are less committed to the idea of marriage, but unlike their peers raised in intact marriages, children of divorce have lower expectations and fewer role models for how to make a marriage work. Indeed, without the positive role model of parents married to each other, children often go on to repeat many of their parent's mistakes and end up getting divorced themselves, even if they have a strong desire for a stable marriage.

Wallerstein remains cautious in her advice to parents, providing the disclaimer that "I don't know of any research, mine included, that says divorce is universally detrimental to children."[28] She also points out that some children describe benefits from the experience, such as becoming more independent and self-sufficient: "Finally, we see that many children of divorce are stronger for their struggles. They think of themselves as survivors who have learned to rely on their own judgment and to take responsibility for themselves and others at a young age."[29]

In the end, she urges parents to consider carefully the decision to divorce and to see it as a last resort. She describes some of the children who were raised in unhappy but intact families. Their parents had very real complaints about their marriage and could have considered divorce, but choose not to:

> Their marriages were not so explosive or chaotic or unsafe that husband and wife felt living together was intolerable. What can we learn from them?...If this describes you, I think you should seriously consider staying together for the sake of your children.[30]

This isn't politically correct advice—it certainly isn't what many men and women want to hear—but it's sound counsel nevertheless.

Conclusion

Women contemplating divorce—and even young women contemplating marriage—should be aware of the problems commonly associated with divorce for children and the divorcees themselves.

This does not mean that women should avoid divorce at all costs. Undoubtedly, there are cases when the benefits to the woman and her children of leaving a troubled relationship outweigh the drawbacks. But it's important for women to be cognizant of the potential problems that she and her children may experience when making that calculated decision of whether to end a marriage that may not be as hopeless as it seems.

Chapter Nine

FERTILITY FACTS

$\mathcal{I}$nfertility affects more than six million Americans or about 10 percent of the reproductive-age population. While many factors affect an individual's reproductive health, age plays a major role in a woman's ability to get pregnant.

Knowing the facts about your health and body is universally recognized as basic common sense. But when it comes to reproduction, politics can override common sense.

Fertility and aging: off-limits in our politically correct culture

In 2001, the American Society of Reproductive Medicine—the largest professional U.S. organization of fertility specialists—launched an ad campaign designed to raise awareness about factors that affect women's fertility. The ads focused on four issues: smoking, sexually transmitted diseases (STDs), being overweight, and age, all of which affect women's ability to conceive.

No one objected to highlighting problems associated with smoking, obesity, and STDs. Age set off a firestorm.

Guess what?

- Many women have been led to believe that they can postpone child-bearing without consequence.

- The organized feminist movement and women's studies programs do next to nothing to address the lack of information about age-related infertility.

- A healthy thirty-year-old woman has a 20 percent chance of getting pregnant in a given month. Ten years later, that forty-year-old has just a 5 percent chance.

New York City buses featured hourglass shaped baby bottles, with milk—representing time—dripping away. The image was certainly provocative. Like most issue ad campaigns, the point was to get women talking about the issue and encourage them to get more information.

The text of the ad was actually quite matter of fact. The headline stated: "Advancing age decreases your ability to have children." The text continued "While women and their partners must be the ones to decide the best time when (and if) to have children, women in their twenties and early thirties are most likely to conceive. Infertility is a disease affecting 6.1 million people in the United States."

The National Organization for Women was outraged. Kim Gandy, NOW's president, complained: "Certainly women are well aware of the so-called biological clock. And I don't think that we need any more pressure to have kids."[1] In an interview conducted at the time of the campaign, Kim Gandy is reported to have "kept adamantly reiterating that there are women in their 40s who have no trouble conceiving, and women in their 20s who just can't seem to make a baby."[2]

In a more carefully crafted reaction to the advertising campaign in an op-ed in *USA Today*, Gandy stressed the importance of women getting information about their health: "NOW commends the good doctors for attempting to educate women about their health, but we think they are going about it in the wrong way—by blaming individual women and their behavior for a problem that is caused by many factors, some behavioral, but most not. The ASRM gets free publicity, and women are, once again, made to feel anxious about their bodies and guilty about their choices."[3]

Gandy doesn't explain how a statement of fact is an attempt to make women feel "guilty" about their choices. The ad simply reminds women that they *are making* a choice when they put off children and that there may be unwelcome consequences. The very essence of making a choice is to understand fully the costs and benefits of each option. Without all

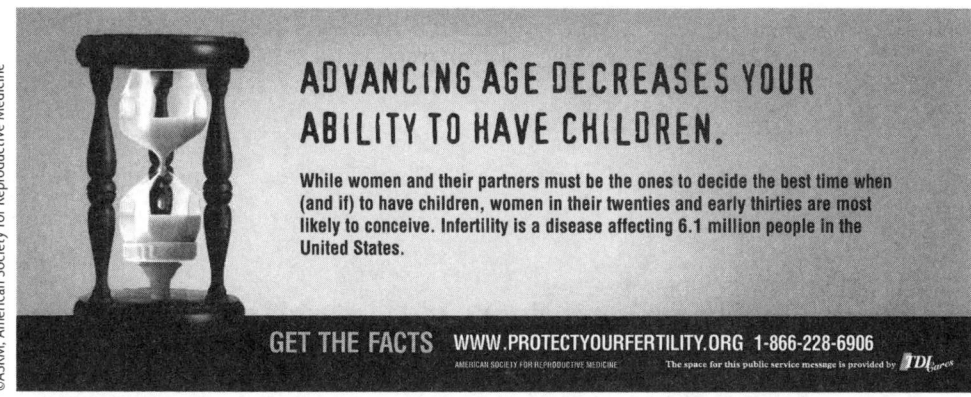

ADVANCING AGE DECREASES YOUR ABILITY TO HAVE CHILDREN.

While women and their partners must be the ones to decide the best time when (and if) to have children, women in their twenties and early thirties are most likely to conceive. Infertility is a disease affecting 6.1 million people in the United States.

GET THE FACTS WWW.PROTECTYOURFERTILITY.ORG 1-866-228-6906

AMERICAN SOCIETY FOR REPRODUCTIVE MEDICINE   The space for this public service message is provided by *TDI Cares*

IF YOU SMOKE THIS MIGHT BE YOUR ONLY USE FOR A BABY'S BOTTLE.

If you smoke, you are most likely aware of the health risks involved. But you probably don't know that smoking can affect your ability to have children. Infertility is a disease affecting 6.1 million people in the United States. Behaviors you engage in before you are ready to have children can impact your future ability to conceive. Smoking can cause infertility in men and women.

GET THE FACTS WWW.PROTECTYOURFERTILITY.ORG 1-866-228-6906

AMERICAN SOCIETY FOR REPRODUCTIVE MEDICINE   The space for this public service message is provided by *TDI Cares*

Guess which one is politically incorrect?

of the relevant information, women may make decisions that don't reflect their true preferences.

There's reason to believe that many women don't recognize the choices they are making when they delay childbirth. In spite of Gandy's accusation that the non-profit was motivated by a desire for "publicity," a spokesman explained that the association wanted to run the ads because doctors were tired of having women in their late thirties and forties shocked, frustrated, and heartbroken to find that their dreams of having children had vanished.

No taboo about smoking's drawbacks

Neither NOW nor any other groups complained about the anti-smoking fertility ad, which was much more hard-hitting. That picture showed a baby bottle being used as an ashtray. The headline gave a stern warning: "If you smoke this might be your only use for a baby's bottle."

When it comes to smoking, no one follows Gandy's logic that because the public already knows about the health hazards there shouldn't be more advertising harping on the problem; or that these issue ads are designed to make smokers "feel guilty" about their choices. The federal government pours money into education campaigns on the dangers of smoking, in spite of research that shows that Americans are well aware of the dangers. Clearly the assumption behind anti-smoking ads is that it takes more than just knowing the facts; those facts have to be repeated many times to change behavior.

It's far from clear that women do know the facts about fertility. Many women have been led to believe that they can postpone childbearing without consequence and regret that decision later in life.

While there are numerous websites and forums that allow women to receive and share information about fertility issues and treatments, the natural decline in fertility is rarely a topic in mainstream women's magazines, particularly among those that cater to a twenty-something audience. The cover of the May 2005 issue of *Marie Claire* includes the alarming headline: "30 & Infertile? Why YOU are at RISK." The story focuses on the difficult to diagnosis condition called premature ovarian failure (POF) that can inflict young women and make them unable to conceive. A similar column in the March 2005 *Cosmopolitan* focused on the plight of a twenty-three-year-old inflicted with POF. These articles are important for raising awareness about health problems among women, and helping women understand the need to monitor their fertility, but does little to encourage the healthy twenty- or thirty-something woman to consider the natural decline in her fertility.

Without Issue

Fertility and aging "is a non-issue."

—Julie Shah, co-director, Third Wave Foundation (a feminist organization representing young feminists)

The March 2005 issue of *Glamour* provides readers with tips on how *not* to get pregnant and how *to* get pregnant, but barely touches on how getting pregnant becomes more difficult with age. Tip number three for how to conceive—"The Importance of Being Healthy"—encourages readers to quit smoking, limit caffeine and alcohol, and achieve a healthy body weight. Age's role in fertility is buried in the last paragraph. A doctor who assures readers "we all know women over forty who got pregnant without aid of technology" before recommending women get started before thirty-five, and at the latest thirty-nine.

Hit television shows have depicted female characters struggling with problems of infertility. On *Sex and the City*, Charlotte undergoes fertility treatments and suffers a miscarriage while attempting to overcome natural fertility obstacles. On *Friends*, Monica and Chandler find that due to a combination of his low sperm count and problems with her womb, they're unlikely to ever get pregnant. In both cases, the couples go on successfully to adopt babies.

While these shows may be helpful in making women aware of the potential for health problems that contribute to infertility, neither characters' situation is a result of age-related fertility.

In general, without good information, women can easily avoid consideration about fertility until they are seriously thinking about having children. By that time, fertility already could be a problem.

Infertility: a "non-issue" for feminists and women's studies

The organized feminist movement and women's studies programs do next to nothing to address the lack of information about age related infertility. Julie Shah, co-director of the Third Wave Foundation (a group representing and promoting young feminists), described fertility and aging as "a non-issue."[4] NOW's centerpiece issue is abortion rights, but information about problems associated with fertility is all but absent on their website.

A sampling of textbooks used by introductory women's studies classes suggests that the subject of fertility is seldom considered. In Virginia Sapiro's textbook *Women in American Society: An Introduction to Women's Studies*, there's a chapter entitled "Reproduction, Parenthood, and Child Care."[5] It covers attitudes toward motherhood, growing availability of contraception, the change in demographics as more women choose to have children later in life, and the challenges of raising children. Twelve pages are dedicated to a discussion of the history and growing availability of contraception, more than half of which is dedicated to abortion. Never in her discussion of women's greater ability to *prevent* childbearing does Sapiro discuss the problems some women face in *not being able* to conceive or carry a child to term.

Hilary M. Lips's *Sex and Gender* dedicates seven pages to women's menstrual cycle and another two pages to exploring the possibility of men having a similar "cycle," but there's no discussion about how age affects women's fertility. After a section on pregnancy, expectant fatherhood, childbirth and the postpartum experience, and abortion, readers begin to read about menopause. The section begins: "At about age 40, women's ovaries begin to stop responding to stimulation by pituitary hormones to produce estrogen and progesterone."[6] After describing some of the physical symptoms experienced during menopause, she mentions the loss of fertility: "A woman at this stage is losing her ability to bear children—an ability that our culture tends to emphasize as crucial to the feminine role."[7]

While Lips may believe our culture is too fixated on women's fertility and that too much value is attached to this ability to bare children, many women personally attach a great deal of importance to having children and are willing to go to great lengthens to get pregnant. Their lack of understanding of the realities of fertility can lead to serious heartbreak and regret.

Facing the facts

The realities of fertility are masked by highly publicized examples of women who are having babies in their forties and beyond. In November 2004, the fifty-five-year-old Ms. Aleta St. James gave birth to twins. This received press attention both in New York where the babies were born, and nationwide. Some stories discussed the hard road this mother had to achieving pregnancy, but others left the story of her conception as an aside. Women's magazines and entertainment television shows often feature celebrities who give birth late in life. Rarely do they discuss the challenge of getting pregnant or the expensive measures that many of these celebrities have taken in order to conceive. But it's critically important that women consider that it took St. James three years and in vitro fertilization treatments that cost $25,000 to create those twins.[8]

Kim Gandy certainly is correct that some women easily get pregnant in their forties while other twenty-somethings struggle with infertility. There are also people who smoke a pack per day and live into their nineties while twenty-year-olds who follow all the rules of a healthy life are tragically struck down by illness. The fact that exceptions exist doesn't mean that women ought to ignore medical research and assume that they will be among the lucky who defy the odds.

So what are the facts about fertility?

According to American Society for Reproductive Medicine, an estimated one in three couples in which the female is over age thirty-five will have fertility problems. By age forty, two out of three women will not be able to achieve pregnancy spontaneously.[9] According to RESOLVE, a woman in her late twenties is about 30 percent less fertile than she was in her twenties.

The American Society for Reproductive Medicine describes how age is associated with a decline in fertility:

> Although the average age of menopause is 51, peak efficiency in the female reproductive system occurs in the early 20s with a steady decline thereafter. There is a gradual loss of fertility as a function of female age with the rate of decline in fertility becoming more dramatic after the age of 35.[10]

A healthy thirty-year-old woman has a 20 percent chance of getting pregnant in a given month. Ten years later, that forty-year-old has just a 5 percent chance of conceiving.[11]

The reason for this decline in fertility is simple. A woman is born with all of the eggs that she will produce during her lifetime. This supply of eggs depletes over time. Her eggs also age, declining in quality so that they are less likely to be successfully fertilized and brought to term.

While conception becomes more difficult as a woman ages, the potential for something to go wrong during pregnancy also increases. Just one in ten women under thirty suffers a miscarriage; by age forty, one in three women will lose their child through miscarriage.

The potential for other problems also rises with age. Older eggs are more likely to contain genetic abnormalities, making the incidence of Down Syndrome or other chromosomal abnormalities more common.[12]

Of course, women confronting fertility problems should know that there are treatments that can help women reproduce. The American Infertility Association's brochure entitled "What Mother Didn't Tell You

About Fertility…Because No One Ever Told Her," contains this comforting statistic: "as many as 90 percent of infertile couples achieve families with the assistance of a vast array of increasingly refined medical therapies and treatments, including oocyte and sperm donation."[13]

However, women need to realize that the effectiveness of these treatments also declines as women age. In vitro fertilization works about one-third of the time in women under age thirty, nearly 30 percent of the time for women in their mid thirties, but just 5 to 15 percent of the time for those over forty years old.[14] Even this statistic may delude some women, since many fertility clinics limit treatment to those under a threshold age, such as forty-four.

Perhaps breakthroughs are around the corner. And some research may indicate that women's prospects for conceiving a child at a given age are slightly better or slightly worse than the numbers from the American Society of Reproductive Medicine. But women should be aware and take into account the basic facts about how their bodies age and their reproductive life diminishes with time. Women may want to monitor medical breakthroughs, but should be cautious in assuming that medicine will be able to alter this reality in time to make a difference for them.

Another one-in-four figure

Gallup found that about one-third of Americans over age forty do not have children and only one-quarter of those say that they would have no children if they had it to do over again.

The consequences of not knowing the facts

If all women were aware of how age affects fertility, then Kim Gandy would have a point that advertisements warning of age-related problems might needlessly torment them. Women choosing to delay childbirth would be taking a calculated risk. Women for whom pregnancy was not an option—due to a lack of a partner or other life circumstances—wouldn't benefit from these reminders, but could be upset by having to confront once again their lack of options.

But surveys suggest that there *is* an information deficiency and that many women are unaware of the factors that affect fertility. The American Infertility Association surveyed 12,383 women and found that 88 percent overestimated by five to ten years the age at which fertility begins to diminish.[15] Nearly half wrongly assumed that general health was an indicator of fertility.

Getting information to these women so that they can make informed decisions is key. Unfortunately, as a result of the initial outcry against the ad campaign in 2001, when the American Society of Reproductive Medicine planned to run these ads again in 2002, shopping malls and movie theaters in San Francisco, Boston, Houston, and Washington, D.C., rejected them. The venues claimed that they preferred "mall friendly" and "happy environment" ad campaigns.

Fertility treatment is a $2.7 billion industry.[16] According to the American Society for Reproductive Medicine, an estimated 300,000 couples are now undergoing treatment for infertility.

Those statistics mask the real heartbreak of this story. In 1998, Sylvia Ann Hewlett set out to write a book "celebrating the achievements of the breakthrough generation—that first generation of women who broke through barriers and became powerful figures in fields previously dominated by men."[17] In the course of conducting interviews, Hewlett discovered that "none of these women had children," and, more disturbingly, "none of these

A Book You're Not Supposed to Read

Creating a Life: Professional Women and the Quest for Children, Sylvia Ann Hewlett; New York, Talk Miramax Books, 2002

women had chosen to be childless."[18] She then changed courses and focused on the issue of childlessness among professional women.

Hewlett interviewed several highly successful women, seeking a better understanding of how they had come to be childless, and described her shock at the extent of their heart-break and feelings of loss from not having children:

> I was taken aback by what I heard. Going into these interviews I had assumed that if these accomplished, powerful women were childless, surely they had chosen to be. I was absolutely prepared to understand that the exhilaration and challenge of a megawatt career made it easy to decide not to be a mother. Nothing could be further from the truth. When I talked to these women about children, their sense of loss was palpable. I could see it in their faces, hear it in their voices, and sense it in their words.[19]

One of these highly successful, childless women described her "creeping nonchoice" of having the potential for children disappear.

In addition to these interviews, in January 2001, Hewlett partnered with Harris Interactive and the National Parenting Association to conduct a survey targeting the top 10 percent of women in terms of earnings in two age groups: twenty-eight to forty and forty-one to fifty-five. The groups were broken down into "high-achievers," who earned over $55,000 or $65,000 depending on age, and "ultra-achievers," who earned in excess of $100,000.

The survey revealed that 33 percent of high-achieving women and nearly half of ultra-achieving women in corporate America were childless at age forty. In contrast, just one-quarter of high-achieving men and 19 percent of ultra-achieving men (earning more than $200,000) were childless at forty.[20]

The survey also confirmed that for most women, the lack of children was not the result of a conscious choice. Women were asked to look back to when they had graduated college and consider whether they had then wanted children. Only 14 percent responded that they had definitely not wanted children at that time. Even among those women who had children, nearly one in four stated that they wanted more children than they were finally able to produce.[21]

Many women had not yet come to terms with the reality that bearing children was likely not in their future. Sadly, almost one-quarter of high-achieving women and one-third of ultra-achievers age forty-one to fifty-five that Hewlett interviewed still hoped to have children. Hewlett concluded: "Given the odds against these midlife women bearing children, these responses point to a mother lode of pain and yearning."[22]

A Gallup poll taken in 2003 found similar evidence of regret among the childless. Gallup found that about one-third of Americans over age forty do not have children and only one-quarter of those say that they would have no children if they had it to do over again. Forty-six percent of childless Americans over age forty wish they had two children, 10 percent wish they had one, and 15 percent would have preferred three or more.[23]

What does this mean for women?

Once a woman has the facts about her fertility, what is she supposed to do? Certainly not every thirty-year-old woman ought to rush out and commence procreating. But women should educate themselves about fertility, not only the role that age plays, but also factors such as sexually transmitted diseases, weight, and smoking. Armed with this information, women should carefully weigh their options and make a plan for how they can best achieve their goals.

One high achieving woman interviewed by Hewlett offered young women this advice:

> Ask yourself what you need to be happy at 45. And ask your-self this question early enough so that you have a shot of get-ting what you want. Learn to be as strategic with your personal life as you are with your career. [24]

That's good advice. In addition to thinking carefully about their own priorities, women should talk to their doctors and other healthcare professionals. They should monitor breakthroughs in medicine, but take care to learn about the limits of new treatments so that they're not overly opti-mistic about their potential effectiveness.

This is a tough issue that will require many women to engage in soul searching and make difficult decisions. But there's no benefit to ignorance or to allowing ourselves to believe that we can put off childbearing with-out consequence. As in most areas of life, information is power, and it's key to helping women to make decisions in their long-term interests.

Chapter Ten

ABORTION

*D*iscussions about abortion typically revolve around questions of morality and whether the procedure is the equivalent of murder. Pro-lifers believe that abortion is the killing of an unborn human being, with rights that merit government protection; pro-choicers believe that abortion is a medical procedure that's critical for women to maintain control of their lives and destinies.

This debate is as critical as it is contentious. Yet it overlooks several important issues surrounding abortion. Conversations about the legality of abortion are also often based on some faulty assumptions. Young women, in particular, tend to receive a one-sided (pro-choice) point-of-view from women's studies programs and media. To have a healthy debate and understanding of the issue, it's important that both sides are properly represented and treated fairly.

This chapter does not attempt to tackle the question of abortion's legality. Instead, it explores some of the incomplete information given to young women about abortion and delves into a few issues rarely covered in the current debate.

Guess what?

- The treatment of abortion in women's studies and the media often begins with the assumption that most young women are—and ought to be— pro-choice.

- When it comes to abortion, European countries often have more restrictive policies than the United States.

- Overturning *Roe v. Wade* would merely move the fight over abortion from the courts and federal arena into state legislatures and referenda.

Pro-life is not anti-woman

Women's studies courses tend to work hand-in-hand with feminist organizations on a political and policy agenda—and abortion rights are at the center of that agenda.

Undoubtedly, it's important for women to understand how changes in the laws governing reproduction have affected them throughout history, and to consider the arguments for keeping abortion legal. Arguments in support of the "pro-choice" position are that control over reproduction gives women the ability to define their lives and control their destinies; women who aren't ready to be mothers—due to their age, the lack of a partner, or alternative life plans—shouldn't have to be; it's cruel to bring children into the world who are going to be poor or unwanted; and finally, since the pregnancy takes place within the woman's body, it's her right to determine whether or not to continue it.

Women are regularly presented with these arguments in support of abortion rights on college campuses and in popular media. But women—particularly students—also need to hear and understand the other side's position.

Unfortunately, in many women's studies textbooks, and in popular media, the pro-life position is rarely articulated or when it is, it's caricatured.

An Introduction to Women's Studies: Gender in a Transnational World contains six essays in the section entitled "Population Control and Reproductive Rights: Technology and Power"—not one represents the pro-life point of view. The section covers how reproductive issues have evolved throughout history, including how advances in reproductive technology have made contraception and abortion more readily available, and the ugly use of coerced abortion and sterilization in the name of population control or based on racism. All of the essays focus exclusively on the rights of the woman. None explores the argument that the fetus or unborn child also has rights.

Issues in Feminism: An Introduction to Women's Studies by Shelia Ruth, contains a more egregious example of distorting the pro-life position as one based on a desire to repress women. Ruth presents the pro-life movement's supposed concern for the fetus as nothing more than a smoke screen:

> The matter of reducing women to "delivery systems," of ignoring the fact that women are people, with needs, feelings, goals, values, even when we are reproducing, is a crucial concept, for it is the heart of the antiabortion issue. It is that, the erasing of our personhood, together with a similar but opposite logical maneuver—the elevation of a fetus to the status of "person"—that makes the antichoice campaign work. It is what makes the rhetoric so effective even though it is often false and misleading....
>
> For several years and with growing intensity, the antifeminist, antichoice advocates have thrown up a smoke screen against their very real agenda: control over women's lives, our self-determination, our right to make decisions for ourselves, and our personal, economic, and social destinies.

What a Feminist Icon Said:

"No matter what the motive, love of ease, or a desire to save from suffering the unborn innocent, the woman is awfully guilty who commits the deed. It will burden her conscience in life, it will burden her soul in death; But oh, thrice guilty is he who drove her to the desperation which impelled her to the crime."

From *The Revolution*, a paper published by Susan B. Anthony and Elizabeth Cady Stanton, quoted by Kate O'Beirne, http://www.nationalreview.com/kob/obeirne200601230842.asp

This is not how most pro-lifers—who generally believe that life begins at conception and that the unborn have rights—would describe their reasons for opposing abortion,

You may disagree with this view and believe that the entity waiting to be born should not be considered fully human, with the right to life until after birth (or upon reaching a certain stage of development, such as being viable outside of the uterus). However, it's worth considering—especially in an educational environment—the arguments of the other side. Surely pro-choice women would object to textbooks that describe their position as motivated by a blood thirst and hatred of children, rather than an honest concern for the rights of women.

The treatment of abortion in women's magazines and media often begins with the assumption that most young women are—and ought to be—pro-choice. The August 2005 issue of *Glamour* contains an article, "The Mysterious Disappearance of Young Pro-Choice Women." It includes a serious examination of the shift in attitudes among young women, a majority of whom had supported unrestricted abortion rights ten years ago and now have greater sympathy for restrictions on abortion. The author considers the factors that have contributed to this trend, including an increased trust in birth control and greater acceptance of the belief that a fetus is a human life, due to the prevalence of sonogram images.

What *Roe v. Wade* Really Says

With respect to the State's important and legitimate interest in potential life, the "compelling" point is at viability. This is so because the fetus then presumably has the capacity of meaningful life outside the mother's womb. State regulations protective of fetal life after viability thus has both logical and biological justifications. If the State is interested in protecting fetal life after viability, it may go so far as to proscribe abortion during that period, except when it is necessary to preserve the life or health of the mother.

—The Opinion of the Court, *Roe v. Wade*, January 22, 1973

The underlying tone of the article suggests that women are mistaken in their shift of support or are deviating from their natural state. They hypothesize that supporting abortion restrictions is a luxury women can afford only because abortion is currently legal and accessible. If that were to change, those who now are critical of abortion would switch back to supporting abortion rights. The article closes by quoting Gloria Feldt, president of Planned Parenthood, who is confident that if *Roe v Wade* were overturned women would once again take to the streets and asks young women, "Why wait?"

The September 2004 issue of *Cosmopolitan* was even less subtle. Under the headline "How Your Rights Are Being Robbed," author Liz Welch details "the assault on women's rights" inherent in the Bush administration's support for pro-life policies. She warns women: "Just as the Supreme Court gave women the right to choose in 1973, it can take it away in 2004. Or 2005." The article closes urging women to vote for pro-choice candidates. Similarly, the April 2004 issue of *Glamour* included a one-page call to arms, "Your Most Fundamental Female Rights—Stand Up for Them," which urged women to participate in the abortion rights rally in Washington, D.C. You can be sure that no similar ink was given in anticipation of any pro-life event.

This one-sided representation of the issue is a disservice to young women. Both pro-life and pro-choice advocates have deeply held beliefs that are based on a moral foundation. Young women should be challenged with the best arguments, not shielded from debate and force-fed propaganda.

Roe v. Wade's real role

Roe v. Wade is the best known Supreme Court case today and abortion's battleground. Protecting or reversing this decision is the focal point for activists on both sides.

In April 2004, an estimated one million women and men descended on Washington, D.C. to participate in a rally organized by feminist groups, including the NOW and the Feminist Majority. The event was held on the National Mall and dubbed "The March for Women's Lives." It was a call to arms to defeat Republicans and President Bush and to defend *Roe v. Wade*—both missions were depicted as vital to the very survival of women.

In discussions about abortion and the role of the Supreme Court, it's important to understand what would really happen if the Court were to reverse *Roe v. Wade*. Contrary to most rhetoric, overturning *Roe* would not make abortion illegal in the United States. It would grant state legislatures and the Congress greater latitude to place or enforce restrictions on abortion. For many American women, the end of *Roe* would have little practical impact.

The Center for Reproductive Rights, the leading advocacy organization for abortion rights, analyzed existing laws in the states and concluded that twenty-one states are "at the highest risk" of having some restrictions on abortion if *Roe* is overturned. Some of these states currently have laws on the books that restrict abortions that would become enforceable if *Roe* is reversed. Others were judged as have state legislatures likely to pass new restrictions. The Center for Reproductive Rights concluded that in twenty states, abortion rights are established in the state constitutions or in statute, and therefore are unlikely to be threatened by new legislative action. They judged the outlook "uncertain" in the remaining nine states.[1]

Other groups see a reversal of *Roe* as having a more limited impact, at least initially. The non-profit Life Legal Defense Fund conducted a similar analysis and concluded that only seven states (Louisiana, Michigan, Oklahoma, Rhode Island, South Dakota, Wisconsin, and Arkansas) have laws on the books that would prohibit abortions and so would be immediately affected by the overturning of *Roe*. In many other states, actions would likely be taken to activate new restrictions.

How Reversing *Roe v. Wade* Would Likely Affect Abortion Access in the 50 States

Abortion Likely Restricted	Abortion Availability Unchanged	Outlook Uncertain
Alabama	Alaska	Arizona
Arkansas	California	Georgia
Colorado	Connecticut	Idaho
Delaware	Florida	Illinois
Kentucky	Hawaii	Indiana
Louisiana	Maine	Iowa
Michigan	Maryland	Kansas
Mississippi	Massachusetts	New Hampshire
Missouri	Minnesota	Pennsylvania
Nebraska	Montana	
North Carolina	Nevada	
North Dakota	New Jersey	
Ohio	New Mexico	
Oklahoma	New York	
Rhode Island	Oregon	
South Carolina	Tennessee	
South Dakota	Vermont	
Texas	Washington	
Utah	West Virginia	
Virginia	Wyoming	
Wisconsin		

Source: The Center for Reproductive Rights

What these analyses ultimately reveal is that in a post-*Roe* scenario, abortion would become predominately a state issue. Federal legislation could be implemented, but most likely it would be up to state legislatures to determine the availability of abortion. Women in more liberal areas of the country—such as the Northeast and West Coast—would be unlikely to face significant restrictions on abortion. Women in states where support for abortion rights is low, such as the Mid-West and South, would likely face new restrictions.

A federalist approach to abortion causes great alarm for many pro-choice women, particularly those in more conservative, "red" states, and gives pro-life women hope that overturning *Roe* could reduce the number of abortions. However, it's important for women on both sides of the debate to understand that overturning *Roe* would not be an end of the fight over abortion; it would merely move that fight from the courts and federal arena into state legislatures and referenda.

Abortions overseas—Europe is not as liberal as you might think

Europe has a reputation of being more socially liberal—supportive of gay marriage, out of wedlock births, and casual sex—than puritanical America. It surprises many to learn that when it comes to abortion, European countries often have more restrictive policies than those currently in place in the United States.

In the United Kingdom, abortion is legal for the first twenty-four weeks of a pregnancy, if continuing the pregnancy involves a greater risk to the health (physical or mental) of the woman or her existing children than does terminating that pregnancy. Abortion is allowed after twenty-four weeks (roughly the fifth month of pregnancy) only if there is a risk to the life of the woman, evidence of a severe fetal abnormality, or risk of "grave" physical and mental injury to the woman. Two doctors must agree to the need for an abortion.[2]

Abortion is illegal in Ireland unless the mother's life is in danger.[3] In Sweden, abortion is allowed only up to week eighteen, after that abortions are limited to "extraordinary circumstances."[4] In France—often touted as the pinnacle of enlightened liberalism—abortion is available up until the twelfth week of pregnancy.[5]

Clearly, Americans are not alone in trying to balance the rights of the unborn with the rights of the woman. While American media tends to depict the U.S. pro-life movement as an outgrowth of the "Religious Right," the same concerns for the life of the fetus are apparent in these more secular European countries.

Abortion as a health issue

Each year, more than one million pregnancies end in abortion.[6] Researchers estimate that between one-third and half of all U.S. women will have an abortion by the time they are forty-five.[7] Fifty percent of all abortions are obtained by women under age twenty-five; one out of five is obtained by a teen.

While abortion is most commonly examined from a moral standpoint, it's also a health issue. If up to half of American women are going to undergo this procedure during their lifetime, it's important to consider what it may mean for their health.

Most research indicates that abortion is generally a safe medical procedure, especially when it's performed in the early stages of pregnancy. According to the Alan Guttmacher Institute, less than 1 percent of all abortion patients experience a major complication, such as infection, hemorrhaging, or damage to the uterus. Women typically experience a number of unwelcome, temporary side effects after undergoing an abortion, including abdominal pain and cramping, nausea, vomiting, and diarrhea.[8]

According to the CDC, in 1998 and 1999, fourteen women died from complications from induced abortions.[9] The risk of death associated with abortion that year was .6 per 100,000 abortions, while the risk of death from child birth was 6.7 per 100,000, or ten times greater.[10]

Abortion Is More Dangerous Than Taking Aspirin

Abortion may be a relatively safe medical procedure, but it still carries physical health risks. This is just one of the reasons that Americans overwhelmingly support laws that would require a minor seeking an abortion to obtain parental consent before doing so. Yet in six states and in Washington, DC, a minor can obtain an abortion without getting permission from a parent, and in many other states, laws that would require minors to obtain parental consent are currently working their way through the courts.

When it comes to many other less serious health issues, parental involvement is expected and required. Most public schools, for example, aren't allowed to provide students with basic over-the-counter medicines, such as aspirin, without a parent's permission. In New Hampshire—where a parental consent law is currently being challenged and reviewed by the Supreme Court—children under age 18 must have a parent's permission to use a tanning machine and those under 14 must have a note from a doctor. Similar restrictions on children's access to tanning machines exist in California, where a child can get an abortion without parental notification. New York has no parental notification requirement when it comes to abortion, but it does have one for a child who wants to get a tattoo or have his or her nose pierced.

See: Kathryn Jean Lopez, "Aborting Parental Rights," National Review Online, June 8, 2005

While this finding may provide comfort to women considering an abortion, it shouldn't be taken as evidence that abortion is no big deal. Abortion is still a painful procedure, with potentially serious consequences. The National Right to Life Committee highlights the finding that 97 percent of women report experiencing pain during abortion and more than one-third describe that pain as intense. The complications that can occur as a result of an abortion can affect future pregnancies and have long term health consequences.[11]

Young women should be aware also of research into a potential link between abortion and higher incidents of breast cancer. Some studies suggest that there could be a relationship that puts women who undergo an abortion at greater risk of developing cancer; other studies have found no correlation. This issue, and the research surrounding it, is controversial. But given that abortion is an elective procedure, it's worth young women knowing of this potential risk to their long-term health.

Just because the risk of long-term health damage or death from an early abortion is low doesn't mean that it isn't a serious health issue. Young women considering abortion—or contemplating sexual intercourse before they're ready for pregnancy—should be aware that abortion is a serious medical procedure that entails real discomfort for the patient and is not without risks.

The health of the mother exception

While *Roe v. Wade* is commonly understood as protecting abortion rights, the judges writing this decision recognized that the state may have an interest in restricting abortion after the fetus is viable, or capable of living on its own outside of the womb. *Roe* also included a caveat that any restriction of abortion may not stop what is necessary to preserve a woman's life or health.

It's pretty clear what that means in terms of preserving a woman's life, but what about her health? "Health" is a murky term because the process of giving birth clearly affects a woman's physical health in the short-term, as well as her mental and emotional health. Another case handed down on the same day as *Roe*, *Doe vs. Bolton*, clarified the definition of health: "The medical judgment may be exercised in the light of all factors—physical, emotional, psychological, familial, and the woman's age—relevant to the well-being of the patient. All these factors may relate to health."[12]

In other words, the definition of health is so broad that the restriction on abortion is essentially meaningless: Just about any abortion could be justified as necessary for "health" reasons.

An Alan Guttmacher Institute survey asked women their reasons for having an abortion; 3 percent of women respondent that a health problem was the reason for terminating the pregnancy. There is no data to distinguish how health was defined in these cases—whether it was related to lasting physical health or if the health issue concerned the mother's emotional or mental health.[13]

There are certainly health conditions that may be complicated by pregnancy. A woman diagnosed with breast cancer while pregnant has a limited ability to treat her condition without endangering the health of the baby. Radiation therapy can lead to complications, premature delivery, and increased risk of birth defects. Some doctors may encourage a woman in this situation to consider abortion so that she can undergo immediate treatment. Women with other conditions, such as sickle cell disease and hypertension, face physical risks during pregnancy.

However, those who support the right of women who face serious physical health risks to opt for an abortion should understand that the definition of "health" used by abortion rights supporters usually is not limited to physical health, but includes more nebulous "mental" health.

An informed choice

Young women should be familiar with the arguments of both those on the pro-life and the pro-choice sides of the abortion issue. Unfortunately, much of the information that young women receive—particularly on campus in courses such as women's studies—present only pro-choice arguments. With abortion, as with all issues, women need more information so that they can make an informed choice consistent with their personal beliefs.

Chapter Eleven

WORK IN THE REAL WORLD

*I*n politically correct TV-land, most women have high powered jobs today: they're lawyers, surgeons, or impeccably dressed advertising executives. In the real world, most women hold less than thrilling—and surprisingly traditional—jobs.

Women are thriving in America's education system and, in the years to come, will increasingly enter into and excel in all industries and professions. But it's important for women to have a realistic idea of the role that work plays in most women's lives.

The feminist working girl fairytale

In the 1988 film *Working Girl*, Melanie Griffith is a secretary struggling to break into the executive suite. She has to overcome challenges like an overbearing boss who steals her ideas, a boyfriend who cheats on her, and the stereotypes that comes with being a "secretary." The story is in many ways a fairytale. But in this modern tale, winning the love of the handsome prince, played by Harrison Ford, is a secondary triumph. Instead of ending with a trip to the altar or even a schmaltzy kiss, the movie closes with Griffith's discovering that she has finally earned the keys to the new version of a palace: a windowed office with a secretary of her own.

Guess what?

- Women have made great strides in the workplace but most women are still working in traditional fields and are motivated by financial need.

- The most frequent occupation for women is secretary or administrative assistant.

- It will surprise few outside of NOW that most women actually find paid work less fulfilling than other, more personal activities.

An example more familiar to today's twenty-somethings will be Rachel Green of *Friends*. In the early episodes, Rachel arrived at Central Perk coffee house to join the rest of the gang as a spoiled rich girl from Long Island who left her fiancé at the altar. She was prepared for no activity other than shopping. She got her first job waitressing at Central Perk, and even when she finally breaks into fashion, she's shown once again making coffee for the boss.

By the end of the series, Rachel has transformed into a high powered fashion executive. When she gives birth to her child, she cuts short her maternity leave out of concern that she's losing prestige within her office. In the concluding episodes, Rachel considers moving to Paris with her baby (away from Ross, the baby's father) for a new job. Even though ultimately Rachel opts to stay in New York (presumably to live happily ever after with Ross and in a higher-paying job), her basic personae is of an ambitious career woman.

Professional women in movies and on television rarely work in the nine-to-five world inhabited by most women. *Legally Blonde* shows the ever-fashionable Elle Woods as a law student tracking down criminals and taking charge in the courtroom. Television legal dramas tell a similar tale: the lawyers are constantly engaged in high stakes battles, bringing the bad guys to justice. In reality, just a fraction of lawyers end up in the courtroom—most of their time is spent performing grueling research and combing through tedious contracts.

What most women do

During the past several decades, women have entered the formal workforce in droves. In 1970, just four out of every ten women were participating in the paid workforce. By 2004, nearly six in ten women were employed—that's an increase of nearly 50 percent and represents millions more women entering the paid labor force.[1]

20 Leading Occupations of Employed Full-time Working Women in 2003

Rank	Occupation	Total Women (in thousands)	% of Women
1	Secretaries and administrative assistants	2692	6.1%
2	Elementary and middle school teachers	1780	4.0%
3	Registered nurses	1650	3.7%
4	Nursing, psychiatric, and home health aides	1144	2.6%
5	Cashiers	1040	2.4%
6	Customer service representatives	1038	2.4%
7	First-line supervisors/managers of office and adm support	984	2.2%
8	First-line supervisors/managers of retail sales workers	938	2.1%
9	Bookkeeping, accounting, and auditing clerks	894	2.0%
10	Receptionists and information clerks	831	1.9%
11	Accountant and auditors	784	1.8%
12	Retail salespersons	765	1.7%
13	Maids and housekeeping cleaners	682	1.5%
14	Secondary school teachers	540	1.2%
15	Waitresses	528	1.2%
16	Teacher assistants	527	1.2%
17	Office clerks, general	511	1.2%
18	Financial Managers	491	1.1%
19	Preschool and kindergarten teachers	476	1.1%
20	Cooks	452	1.0%
	Total Percent		**42.5%**

Source: Bureau of Labor Statistics

The increase is even more dramatic among younger women: 72 percent of women between the ages 25 to 54 are now in the paid workforce.[2] This includes a majority of the women with young children: In 2002, 65 percent of women with children under age six were employed.[3] This is

What a Feminist Icon Said:

"I like the idea of young women being mothers. It is easier to get down on the floor with kids if you are a kid yourself."

—Germaine Greer supporting young mothers, who place motherhood ahead of their careers

http://www.cathnews.com/news/208/86.php

nearly the double the portion of mothers with children under six (34 percent) who were working in 1975.[4]

While many events contributed to this social trend, the women's movement played a critical role in encouraging the change. Betty Friedan's watershed book, *The Feminist Mystique*, challenged women to consider taking on roles outside of housewife and mother. Feminists fought against social biases that prevented women from competing and succeeding in fields like medicine, science, politics, and the law. Today, their success is obvious: Women are thriving in industries and professions that just a few decades ago were almost exclusively the domain of men.

Women are now earning more than half of all bachelor's degrees and master's degrees, and 40 percent of doctoral degrees. They also earn four in ten degrees in medicine and nearly half of all law degrees. This academic achievement indicates that women will play a significant role in these prestigious fields in the years to come. But already, women are fast becoming leaders in the new economy. There are more than 8.5 million women-owned businesses in the United States.

Women have made great strides in the workforce and will continue to do so in the future. But it's important to remember that when we talk about working women, most are working in traditional fields and are motivated by financial need.

According to the Bureau of Labor Statistics, the most frequent occupation for women is secretary or administrative assistant. The top twenty professions for full-time working women—which together employ more than 40 percent of all full-time working women—are strikingly traditional, including elementary school teachers, nurses, cashiers, and waitresses.[5] Lawyers and physicians/surgeons don't make the list: Each profession employs well below half the number of women as the twentieth most frequent profession, which is serving as a cook.

Many women employed in these occupations find their jobs personally fulfilling and work because they love it, not simply out of necessity. But this list of occupations stands in stark contrast to the depiction of working women commonly found on television and in women's magazines.

Women's greatest source of fulfillment: not their jobs

Given this reality, it's not surprising that many women—in particular women with children—are ambivalent about their jobs. In 1996, the Independent Women's Forum commissioned a poll that asked the question: "If you had enough money to live as comfortably as you'd like, would you prefer to work full time, work part time, do volunteer work, or work at home caring for your family?" One third replied that part-time work would be their ideal. Nearly another third preferred staying home with children. Twenty percent said ideally they'd do volunteer work and just 15 percent wanted to work full-time.[6]

The Pew Research Center for the People & the Press received a similar response when they surveyed 1,101 American women in 1997 on contemporary motherhood. They asked mothers of children under age eighteen if in their ideal situation they would prefer to work full-time, part-time or not at all. Part-time was the number one choice for these women, earning 44 percent of the responses. Three in ten preferred to work full-time. But in reality, more than half of these mothers were working full-time or more than they would prefer. [7]

It will surprise few outside of NOW that most women actually find paid-work less fulfilling than other, more personal activities. Responses to the Pew survey clearly indicate that women who value time with love ones over their careers are acting rationally in terms of promoting their long-term happiness. Women, regardless of their living situation, rate relationships with loved ones as their greatest source of personal happiness and fulfillment.

Work, on the other hand, is disproportionately responsible for women's frustrations. Two out of ten women responded to the Pew survey that their jobs were frustrating all or most of the time and another 50 percent were frustrated at least some of the time. Jobs were still a source of happiness for 60 percent of working women—but that makes careers the least consistent source of happiness of all the aspects of life included in the poll.

No doubt some of the work-related frustrations that women face are a byproduct of having to juggle work responsibilities with family duties. The Pew survey also found women frustrated by the lack of affordable, quality daycare. The fact that women with higher incomes derive more satisfaction from their jobs also suggests that as women continue to invest in education and obtain higher level positions, jobs may become a more satisfying part of their lives. But these responses suggest that for most women, family and relationships will eclipse career as the top priority during their lives.

Feminists often try to deny this reality. Their misconceptions or unwillingness to recognize the roles that work and family play in real women's lives are more than just an annoyance, with feminists grandstanding about women's oppression. They have serious policy implications. Feminists push policymakers to embrace programs and regulations designed to drive women into the workforce, even if that isn't what women want.

Chapter Twelve

THE MYTH OF HAVING IT ALL

Young women have been taught from the time they were born that all doors are open to them: They can be astronauts, political leaders, athletes, or financial tycoons. The fact that today women have so many choices in life is worth celebrating.

But having choices requires making choices. Reaching the heights of professional or political success requires a great deal of dedication and sacrifice. Women and men both face tradeoffs and must decide how they're going to spend their time.

Women, who bear children and traditionally serve as primary caregivers to their offspring, often feel they face different choices and tradeoffs than men. This may be partly due to societal expectations, but biology and women's strong impulse to nurture their children surely plays a role. Whatever the reasons are, women and men are often going to make different choices about how to prioritize their time.

Feminist groups like to pretend that women can have it all—work fulltime and become leaders of industries, without sacrificing time with families. It's politically incorrect to suggest that one of these areas of life has to come at the expense of, or have an impact on, another.

Yet life involves trade-offs. A gangbuster career typically requires long hours and other inconveniences, like travel and relocation—sacrifices

Guess what?

- Feminist groups like to pretend that women can have it all without sacrificing time with families. This is false and most women know it.

- As surveys indicate, many women sincerely *want* to spend more time with their families.

- Many women don't want to have to work outside of the home and do so only out of financial necessity.

many women don't want to make. That's not a problem that needs solving. So long as women are making choices based on their own preferences, their choices deserve respect.

Feminist frustrations about what women really want

Feminists are often irritated when women choose family over career. In the book *Not Guilty! The Good News for Working Mothers*, Betty Holcomb describes with some alarm an essay written by a Harvard sophomore who felt as though she faced a crossroads—one path marked career and the other marked home life—and felt pulled toward home.

The Harvard undergrad wrote that she knows what it will take to make it to the top of her profession—long hours and complete dedication—and isn't sure if it's the course she wants to follow or if she'd rather reserve more time for her family:

> If I want to succeed, I mean really succeed, in my career, then I have to throw myself into it, heart and soul. I have to be the one working overtime so I will be eligible for promotion. I have to bring home work if need be. I have to travel if that's what it takes. No matter what career I decide upon, I have to give it my all.

This young woman's recognition of the dedication a top career requires and the tradeoffs that she will face is disturbing to Betty Holcomb. Holcomb complains that these subjects set off "urgent, personal questions that have become the stuff of late-night heart-to-hearts" and that "All too often, the conversation is infused with, and confused by, assumptions about gender."[1]

These young women are engaged in important soul-searching about life's priorities in these late-night heart-to-hearts. None of the women cited in her book were suggesting that they *couldn't* have fulfilling work lives while having families, but these women recognized that they may not want to do what it takes and make the sacrifices necessary to reach the highest levels of their professions.

In fiercely defending women's right to work, Holcomb places the blame for the conflicts between work and home on society:

> No serious researcher denies that real conflicts exist between work and family duties today, but the point is that they are not inherent to women's expanding roles. They are not inevitable. Instead, they result from the hostility working moms face on every front. And the old and false stereotype about what makes a good worker and a good mother serve to encourage some of the darkest treatment women face as they try to earn a decent living and raise their children.[2]

Contrary to what Holcomb asserts, conflicts *are* inevitable: There's no way to eliminate the problem that there are only twenty-four hours in a day and that women cannot be two places at once. Women are going to face a choice between spending more of their day at work or more of their day at home, and there inevitably will be consequences.

Feminists sometimes resent that people have the choice to devote (and be rewarded for devoting) significant extra hours to their jobs. Yet women are fortunate to live in a time when the choice

A Milestone in Feminist History

"Well I just wanted to let you know that sometimes I get concerned about being a career woman. I get to thinking that my job is too important to me. And I tell myself that the people I work with are just the people I work with. But last night I thought what is family anyway? It's the people who make you feel less alone and really loved." [she sobs]

—Mary Richards, *The Mary Tyler Moore Show*

between working and staying at home has become much less mutually exclusive. Technology is making working from home efficient and effective. Companies are increasingly offering employees more flexible schedules through programs like comp-time and flex-time. Both make the choice between working and staying at home less difficult.

Still, there will be tradeoffs forever in balancing career with other interests, including family. It will be always hard for someone opting for a flexible arrangement or reduced work week to compete with someone willing to devote all their waking hours to the job. The man or woman who wants to give the extra effort deserves the additional rewards that come with additional work—just as the person who opts to spend more time on outside interests will be rewarded with the fulfillment that these bring.

Athletes face similar calculations. A young runner may show great promise, enjoy competing in the sport, and have the potential to make it to the Olympics. Yet only a select few are willing to do what it takes— put in grueling hours of training at great personal expense and forgo the pleasures associated with a more "normal" life—to make it to the Olympics. Those who choose not to make those sacrifices can still have a rewarding experience running, but they can't complain that they won't get the national television coverage and financial rewards received by the dedicated few who make it to the Olympics and win gold medals.

The same dynamic is true in business. People willing to put in extra hours and devote themselves fully to their profession will usually rise higher than those who take on outside responsibilities or activities— whether those outside activities are children or community service or competitive dog training. Young women are wise to consider how they envision allocating their time between family and career. We should strive to ensure that young women know that all options are open to them, but it's wrong to tell them that there aren't any tradeoffs between work and family.

Wage gap wars

Many feminists refuse to recognize that women and men make different choices when it comes to work and family. These choices lead to different outcomes. It's politically correct to blame these different outcomes on discrimination.

Consider the feminists' concern over the so-called wage gap. The Department of Labor collects multitudes of data and compiles statistics that provide a snapshot of the occupations that Americans work in and how much they are paid. None receives more attention than the statistic that compares the median income of a full-time working woman to that of a full-time working man. Typically, the government finds that the average working woman makes about three-quarters of that of the working man.

If you accept that all women are professionally identical to men—working in the same jobs, and dedicating just as much time and energy to their occupations—then this statistic is a call to arms. Women are being discriminated against and something needs to be done now!

Liberal politicians are responding to this call to arms. Former presidential candidate, Senator John F. Kerry, highlighted how he thinks the government needs to take action to address the vexing problem of the wage gap in a debate during the 2004 campaign. Each year, feminist groups hold events and rallies on "Equal Pay Day." In 2005, it was April 19th and Senator Hillary Clinton was among the speakers at the rally to raise awareness about women's oppression as evidenced by the wage gap. According to feminists, Equal Pay Day is the day that women have finally worked enough in the new year to make up for last year's wage gap.

The Department of Labor statistic used as the basis for this hoopla ignores the many relevant factors that affect a worker's take-home pay. For starters, it doesn't adjust for number of years worked. On average, women spend about a decade out of the workforce caring for their

Red Scare

The National Committee for Pay Equity, which organizes Equal Pay Day events, urges activists to:

Wear RED on Equal Pay Day to symbolize how far women and minorities are "in the red" with their pay!

families. It should come as no surprise that a thirty-five-year-old woman reentering the workforce after ten years off earns less than a man or woman who worked continuously during that time.

The wage-gap statistic also fails to consider educational attainment. Today, women earn more than half of all bachelor's and master's degrees, but it wasn't always that way. Older women in the workforce tend to have less education than their male peers, which affected their career path, their salaries, and ultimately Department of Labor data.

Women and men in general also have different priorities when assessing employment opportunities. One survey of working women found that for nearly three-quarters a flexible schedule was "very important" when considering a job. This means that many women are willing to trade more money for more flexibility or time off.[3]

Gender warriors at the Feminist Majority and NOW lament that women still sacrifice their careers to take on a disproportionate share of childcare responsibilities. But as surveys indicate, many women sincerely *want* to spend more time with their families. And regardless of whether it's out of duty or desire full-time working women tend to spend less time in the office than full-time working men. The Department of Labor time-use study revealed that a full-time working woman spends a half hour, or 7 percent, less time in the office on an average work day than the typical full-time working man.[4]

Several studies that took these factors into account found a considerably smaller wage gap between men and women. One study focused on childless men and women aged twenty-seven to thirty-three and found that women in that group earned ninety-eight cents for every male dollar.

Warren Farrell, a former board member of NOW's New York chapter, wrote a book called *Why Men Earn More* that dissects the decisions that individuals make when choosing a career and individual jobs.[5] He identifies twenty-five decisions that individuals make about work and reveals how, on average, men tend to make decisions that increase their pay, while women do not always opt for the highest paying alternative. In addition to women taking more time out of the labor force and working fewer hours than men, women tend to opt for jobs that require less travel and are less likely to move for a job. Men take on more high risk jobs—they account for 92 percent of deaths that occur in the workplace—and jobs that require braving the elements outdoors.[6]

Recognizing these tradeoffs empowers women to make more money and frees them from the sense that they're automatically victims of discrimination. In identifying the factors affecting earnings, Farrell lays out a roadmap for how women can increase their pay if they want to achieve parity with men. In doing so, he also highlights the tradeoffs that individuals must make. Higher pay typically comes with a price—whether it's taking greater physical risks, spending more time on the road, or logging extra hours in the office. Once you realize that you *could* make more money, but are unwilling to do what it takes to earn those extra dollars, you feel better about the situation that you face.

If you still aren't convinced that "75 cents on the dollar" is a misleading statistic, consider what its veracity would mean. If women perform the same work as men for three-quarters of the pay, then a company that hired only women would have a huge advantage over its competitors. Its fixed employment costs would be much lower for the same amount of output. Sexism in the marketplace would have to be so strong that other companies would rather lose businesses and have higher labor costs—

maybe go bankrupt—rather than to hire more female employees. To believe that a huge persistent wage gap exists is to believe that American businesses—including those run by women—are economically foolish.

The market would not tolerate such foolishness. Certainly some women experience discrimination and are treated unfairly, which affects their pay and these statistics. But the feminist insistence that this wage gap is the result of pure discrimination ignores the real choices that American women make about their careers.

Why do we want women to work like men?

It's important to understand the causes of the wage gap, but it's equally important to recognize why achieving parity on this artificial measure is a nonsensical goal. Why would we expect or want men and women to exhibit exactly the same preferences for work?

If some women want to forgo more dollars for more time with family, then the "wage gap" that results isn't a problem—it's just a number. Attempts to "fix" the perceived problem could make women worse off. For example, feminists groups push for regulations that would force businesses to report to the Equal Employment Opportunity Commission their processes for setting and adjusting wages. But how would businesses respond under this new regime? To comply with this regulation and avoid the threat of government action, many employers would no longer offer the very kinds of flexible work arrangements most appealing to many women. They would

A Book You're Not Supposed to Read

Why Men Earn More: The Startling Truth Behind the Pay Gap—and What Women Can Do About It, Dr. Warren Farrell, Ph.D; New York, AMACOM, 2005.

require all workers to be in the office from precisely nine to five and receive the same compensation. Those who want to negotiate a different contract—working fewer hours or from home—may find it more difficult to find a job.

The feminist dream of fifty-fifty in all walks of life may never happen. If women on average don't want to spend their lives fighting to climb the corporate ladder, then feminists should respect that decision and not force them to take on roles that ignore their true preferences.

Instead of assuming that women are making poor choices and designing public policies to make women act more like men, Warren Farrell challenges his readers to consider that women are making rational choices when they opt not to maximize their incomes:

> Here's the pay paradox that *Why Men Earn More* explains: Men earn more money, therefore men have more power; and men earn more money, therefore men have less power (earning more money as an obligation, not an option). The opposite is true for women: Women earn less money, therefore women have less power; and women earn less money, therefore women have more power (the option to raise children, or to not take a hazardous job).... Low pay makes us feel powerless unless we are conscious of the decisions that we make to accept low pay as a trade-off for the slice of life we receive in return. Then we feel powerful and happy, rather than angry because we feel like victims of discrimination.[7]

Feminists should trust that women are making choices in their best interests and stop complaining about the outcomes revealed in meaningless statistics like the "wage gap." After all, most women know that money isn't everything.

More women working isn't reason to celebrate

Women's increasingly prominent role in the economy is often celebrated as defacto evidence of progress for women. I began the preceding chapter with much the same assumption.

But the reality is that many women don't want to have to work outside of the home and do so only out of financial necessity. They would prefer to spend their time raising their children and contributing to their communities.

Instead of pursuing public policies that facilitate women's increased entrance into the workforce—such as providing subsidized childcare and regulating businesses—policymakers should consider how to create an environment that allows women to make choices that reflect their preferences. For many women that may mean working less and spending more time with their children.

Chapter Thirteen

DAYCARE DELUSIONS

nxiety about women working isn't really about women. It's about children. Some women's groups would have you believe that the anxiety surrounding women's migration into the workplace is that men just aren't comfortable with women in positions of power. Nor do they want to compete with women for jobs or watch their language around the ladies. And, sure, there's some truth in this: A few men want to go back to a largely mythical world where offices were like locker rooms and women were just a part of the decorating scheme.

If it were just about having a few more women in the office and a few less meals waiting for men when they get home, however, this cultural breeze would have passed quickly. It's a storm because children are at its center.

Women with children don't just enter the workforce. They also leave home and, in doing so, must find alternative arrangements for caring for their children. The almost constant needs of infants and toddlers must be attended to by someone else—either a daycare provider or another family member. School age children have to return to an empty house or spend the afternoon at an after-school program when mom's not at home.

Of course, dad has a role to play in this equation too, and fathers are taking a greater role in caring for their children.

Guess What?

- Feminists recoil at research suggesting that children with parents as primary caregivers are better off than those in full-time daycare.

- The type of daycare most often pushed by feminist groups and the government— institutional daycare—is the type of care least popular with parents.

- People generally believe that parents and family members or close friends do a better job caring for their children.

151

But traditionally, women have been the primary caregivers for their children, and most mothers, including working mothers, continue to want this role. As women leave home for the workforce, they must rely on others to assume these responsibilities while they are gone. What's the effect of this major social change in the lives of children?

It's an important question and one that is difficult to answer. Researchers face an uphill battle in isolating daycare's affects from the numerous other factors that impact children's lives. It's also an ideological powder keg.

Feminists recoil at research suggesting that children with parents as primary caregivers are better off than those in full-time daycare. They may not like it, but we need to have an open and honest discussion about the effects of daycare on children. And while it isn't politically correct to say so, the weight of the evidence shows that children cared for by their parents tend to be slightly better off, in terms of behavior and attachment, than their peers in daycare—particularly when the quality of that care is low.

This doesn't mean that all mothers need to quit their jobs and head home to their children, but women should be aware of the research when making decisions about childcare arrangements.

The politically correct position: more government funding of institutional daycare

Questioning daycare's effects on children is commonly characterized as an attack on working women. Feminist groups and women's studies programs often cite the federal government's lack of support for daycare as evidence of an unwillingness to promote women's equality. They see the societal norm of women taking on the role of primary caregiver for children as a product of patriarchy.

For example, the women's studies text-book *Thinking About Women* takes as a given that existing norms that place women at the center of caring for children are wrong-headed, unnatural, and anti-woman.[1] The section on childcare closes by highlighting how families are "an ideological concept" and the nexus for numerous problems, and calls for new policies to support child care, given the new realities of family life.[2]

A Book You're Not Supposed to Read

Home-Alone America: The Hidden Toll of Day Care, Behavioral Drugs, and Other Parent Substitutes, Mary Eberstadt; New York, Sentinel, 2004.

Similarly, another women's studies textbook, *Women in American Society*, considers the lack of institutional support for childcare outside of the home as part of the male-dominated political system that keeps women down:

> Many family policies are implemented to affect men as little as possible. Consider the case of childcare. In a family headed by a two-career married couple, child care is usually primarily the woman's responsibility. It is the woman, not the man, whose job is understood to create the need for child care. Child care centers and baby-sitters are thought to be related to the structure of the woman's time and responsibilities, not men's. . . .
>
> Of course, male-dominated political systems are slow to develop policies that benefit women because such policies often incur new costs to men. . . . If family- and employment-related policies charge women with primary responsibility for child care, men have more freedom to engage in activities outside the home and to make their own independent decisions than they do under policies supporting egalitarian divisions of family labor.[3]

For leftist women's studies teachers, there's no debate about the policies that *should* be pursued in terms of childcare for American children. European-style socialism is the ideal model; the U.S. system is called the "stingiest such program among the leading industrialized nations," and is depicted as blatantly anti-woman.[4]

This sentiment is echoed by feminist organizations and politicians on the Left. When she was First Lady, Hillary Clinton made the case for increased government involvement in childrearing in her book, *It Takes a Village*. The chapter entitled "Child Care Is Not a Spectator Sport," opens with a description of utopian childcare—socialist France:

> Imagine a country in which nearly all children between the ages of three to five attend preschool in sparkling classrooms, with teachers recruited and trained as child care professionals. Imagine a country that conceives of child care as a program to "welcome" children into the larger community and "awaken" their potential for learning and growing.
>
> It may sound too good to be true, but it's not. When I went to France in 1989 as part of a group studying the French child care system, I saw what happens when a country makes caring for children a priority. More than 90 percent of French children between ages three and five attend free or inexpensive preschools.... Even before they reach the age of three, many of them are in full-day programs....
>
> It is no wonder that so many French parents—even mothers who do not work outside the home—choose to send their children to these government-subsidized centers.[5]

Clinton goes on to acknowledge that the United States can't adopt the French system wholesale; it has the notable downside of requiring generous financial support from taxpayers. However, she makes it clear that government should take a much more active role in regulating child care and subsidizing daycare centers to make them the choice of more parents.

Only those who dislike children, want to stunt their development, and keep women down would oppose government provided childcare—or so the story goes from much of the Left. One women's studies textbook goes so far as to link many conservatives' reluctance to have government intervene in matters such as childcare as support for wife beating and child abuse.[6]

Government's role in the mommy wars

Opposing the creation of government funded daycare system is hardly akin to supporting child abuse. Opposition is based on a concept of fairness: Families who want to keep a parent home with their children shouldn't have to pay taxes to support daycare for other people's children.

Government intervention into the area of childcare is the number one battleground of the so-called "mommy wars," or the perceived conflict between the interests of working and stay-at-home moms. Feminists push for policies that reduce the costs of paid childcare, which feels like an attack on the value of the stay-at-home mom. After all, if outside daycare is free for families, then what value is the stay-at-home mom providing? Since she can be replaced at no cost, it becomes more difficult—even for families that believe parents provide superior care—to continue to forgo that second income. The implicit message of free or subsidized daycare is that women should get out of the house, turn their kids over to the professionals, and hit the pavement.

Of course, childcare is never free, even if it's provided at no charge to the user. Taxpayers would have to pick up the tab. And as tax rates rise to pay for these services, it becomes harder for a family to survive on just one income, forcing many women who would prefer to stay home to enter the paid workforce.

Brian Robertson, author of *Day Care Deception: What the Child Care Establishment Isn't Telling Us*, described the dynamic this way:

> The so-called "mommy wars" are not simply the result of over-heated rhetoric on both sides of the day care debate; they are a natural consequence of the fact that the increasing push for national day care comes at the expense of mothers at home—and those who would rather be at home.[7]

There are already policies in place that reflect this bias in favor of parent substitutes. The dependent care tax credit allows families to deduct a portion of employment-related expenses. The value of the credit can be up to $720 for one child or $1,440 for two or more children.[8] The woman who has provided daycare on her own, forgoing outside income, gets nothing from this policy.

What childcare arrangement do women actually want?

Ironically, the type of care most often pushed by feminist groups and the government is the type of care least popular with parents. According to the Survey of Income and Program Participation in 1993—the most recent data available—nearly half of the almost ten million children under age five were being cared for by relatives while their mothers worked. Most of those children were under the care of either grandparents or their fathers. Twenty-one percent were cared for by "non-relatives," including family day care providers or in-home baby centers. Just 30 percent were in organized daycare facilities, or what is sometimes referred to as institutional care.[9]

In 2000, the polling firm, Public Agenda, conducted a survey of 815 parents of children under age five, as well as focus groups and interviews with employers, children's advocates, and those in the child care field and issued a report called "Necessary Compromised." The survey results from the parents revealed an even more striking preference for parental care.

When asked the questions, "Which would you say is the best child care arrangement during a child's earliest years: to have one parent stay at home; to have both parents work different shifts so one is almost always at home; to have a nanny or babysitter at home; to have a close relative look after the child; to bring the child to a mom in the neighborhood who cares for children in her home; or to place a child in a quality day care center," 70 percent of respondents thought it was best for one parent to be at home. Another 14 percent preferred both parents working different shifts. Just 6 percent thought a "quality day care center" was the best arrangement for kids.

In another question, parents overwhelmingly listed daycare as their "least preferred option." More than seven in ten parents of children under five agreed with the statement "parents should only rely on a day care center when they have no other option."

Certainly many parents surveyed thought there was a role for daycare. Parents overwhelmingly understood, and sympathized

We're the government and we've come to help

Most parents of young children say that they themselves, not the government or employers or society in general, should bear the primary responsibility for child care. Few parents spontaneously propose that government offer additional services or subsidies to help them, and few voice resentment about career or financial trade-offs that they may make during their children's early years. Just 1 in 5 say making child care more affordable is a higher priority than alternatives such as improving schools, expanding health coverage or lowering taxes.

Public Agenda, *Necessary Compromises*

with those for whom daycare was a necessity. Many voiced support and concern for single parents and believed that daycare, including programs like Head Start, should be available and could help children from lower income families. And the majority of those currently relying on daycare for their youngest child were satisfied with their arrangement, even though it was not their expressed ideal.

Overall this survey reveals that most parents think that having a parent stay at home is the best way to raise a child; very few are clamoring for government intervention in childcare; and, even fewer embrace the feminist vision of universal government funded institutional care as the ideal for raising children in the United States.

Is it guilt or good mothering?

Why are so many women reluctant to use institutional daycare? Mostly because people generally believe that parents and family members or close friends do a better job caring for their children. The Pew survey found that all women, including those who worked, believed children were better served by having a parent at home when they are young:

> Only 29 percent think that when both parents work full time they can often do a good job of child raising. The same small proportion says that most single mothers can do a good job. Tellingly, only 41 percent of mothers who work full time are confident that such situations are good for children. Women, whether or not they work, believe the more traditional setting, in which the father works full time and the mother stays home, is best for raising children. Twice as many women say the increased number of mothers entering the workplace is bad, rather than good, for society (41 percent to 17 percent).[10]

Similarly, Public Agenda found that parents' preference for parental care was rooted in a belief that parents are best positioned to provide care and that daycare centers simply cannot be trusted to devote as much attention to the child.

The preference for parents to stay-at-home could be an outgrowth of nothing more than tradition or the working mother's sense of inadequacy, fueled by (unnecessary) guilt. Books have been written in an attempt to extinguish the guilt women may feel when they work and make the case that society needs to do a better job in helping them. Consider this quote from *Not Guilty! The Good News for Working Mothers*: "Each day, in large ways and small, they [working mothers] find their choices scrutinized, their motivation under attack, the well-being of their children constantly called into question."[11]

Similarly, Joan K. Peters, in *When Mothers Work: Loving Our Children Without Sacrificing Ourselves*, highlights how working women are blamed for their children's problems and calls on society to update its view of the role of mother:

> We now presume that the common cause of all children's woes is their mother's work, which prevents full-time nurturing. Meanwhile, we ignore the more complicated root cause: our failure to modernize motherhood, to restructure family and change society along with the changing character of women's lives.[12]

These books are essentially a defense of working mothers and call on society to support, instead of condemn, the reality that women are increasingly in the workforce and less available to care full-time for their children.

They highlight research showing that children can thrive in daycare, some better than under the constant care of their mothers. However, most of these books focus on the importance of work in mother's lives, in terms of helping to achieve balance and maintain a separate identity, and argue that these benefits pay dividends to her children. As Holcomb emphasizes:

> the idea that children inevitably suffer when mothers work, that women's interests and children's interests are at odds, has gained wide acceptance. So has the notion that women are inevitably exhausted and depleted when they try to combine a job and family duties. But these ideas are just plain wrong.[13]

A politically correct defining moment: Dr. Spock

…in *A Better World for Our Children: Rebuilding American Values*, Dr. Spock casually suggests that "it is particularly desireable" for parents to spend time with children during the first three years—a far cry from his original insistence that mothers being with their children "as much as possible" during these crucial years is a "necessity." Spock has explained his change of phrasing with surprising candor:

> "I'm scared of going out too strongly for "You should stay home!" because in early editions of *Baby and Child Care* I hinted at that by saying "the early years are very crucial, and maybe you should postpone the advantages of earning a living." And women pounced on me, [saying,] "You made me feel very guilty!" But I noticed they went off to work anyway even if they felt guilty, and that's…the worst of all possible arrangements. So I just tossed it out. It's a cowardly thing that I did; I just tossed it in subsequent editions."

Brian C. Robertson, *Day Care Deception: What the Child Care Establishment Isn't Telling Us*

In defending daycare's effects on children, Holcomb works to minimize the impact a mother's absence will have on her children: "In many cases, a job will have far less significance in a child's life than, say, a family move, marital problems, or a parent suffering from depression." This acknowledges that a mother's absence *can* be traumatic for children—similar to marital strife or parent's illness—things that we tend to hope children can avoid. She emphasizes the benefits that additional income can bring a family, and that most children, regardless of the circumstances in which they are raised, turn out just fine.

All of that's true. No researcher I'm familiar with says that daycare *will* cause serious problems for *most* children. But that doesn't mean that women should ignore research on the potential impact of daycare, or any other arrangements for raising their children. Women in particular read regularly research on the benefits of the latest dietary trend or exercise regime, or of the need to steer children away from exposure to this chemical or that, even when the risks are extremely small. It's equally important for women to be informed about the potential impact of where their children spend their days.

The muzzle on daycare critics

Daycare is such a politically charged issue that it's difficult to get an honest assessment of the latest research. Brian C. Robertson argues persuasively that a different standard is applied to studies critical of institutional daycare. He describes the fall from grace of one researcher, Jay Belsky. Belsky had initially won praise for his research in the late 1970s and early 1980s, which found organized daycare was not associated with negative effects on children. But when additional research caused him to question his initial findings and to conclude that daycare was associated with negative outcomes, he found himself and his research under fierce fire.[14]

Belsky highlighted the hypocrisy of his critics, who dismissed his findings by claiming that the effects were small and did not appear in a majority of children, but had championed results of a similar magnitude when their preferred finding was confirmed: quality of care has an impact on children.[15] He concluded: "Quality of care matters . . . and so does quantity. The latter part seems to be an intolerable truth."[16]

Robertson details other researchers who have changed their tunes about daycare in reaction to the backlash against those who criticize institutional care. T. Berry Brazelton, an expert on child development, initially suggested that early separation from parents could have detrimental affects on children and recommended avoiding it when possible. But in subsequent additions of his book, he removes this advice and apologizes for "adding to mothers' guilt" about not staying home. According to Robertson, Brazelton does not cite new evidence that refutes his previous position, but acts out of a fear of offending some parents by mentioning inconvenient facts.[17]

Dr. Benjamin Spock did a similar about face. Robinson highlights how Dr. Spock went from arguing unambiguously for the importance of mothers caring for their children to downplaying their importance, so as not to offend parents. Similarly, daycare researchers—including those at prominent government institutions, like The National Institute of Child Health and Human Development, which receive millions of dollars from taxpayers to conduct research on these issues—admit their reluctance to give bad news about childcare. As NICHD investigator Robert Rianta explained: "There's more caution in drawing implications that might be worrisome to parents."[18]

The research on daycare: some negative effects on kids

Parents need to hear about the effects of daycare so that they can make informed decisions. The weight of the evidence suggests that children placed in daycare centers for long periods of time are more likely to exhibit problems, including behavioral and attachment disorders, than peers who are raised at home. However, children in higher quality daycare are less likely to suffer any ill effects, and may enjoy some benefits from increased socialization

The NICHD studied data on childcare to determine the relationship between the amount of non-maternal care during the first 4.5 years of life and children's behavior. They cite studies that have showed that reliance on "non-maternal care arrangements" predicted increased behavior problems, especially aggressive behavior, among three- and four-year-olds.[19]

NICHD is careful to note that not all research replicates these results and some research suggests positive effects from center-based care. But the NICHD study goes on to detail evidence that greater aggression during school years is linked to extensive child care, and that "more time in care predicts less harmonious mother-infant interaction and less sensitive mothering."[20]

From NICHD's own study of children in ten geographic sites who were followed from birth to kindergarten, they found similar results in terms of an association between greater amount of non-maternal care and behavioral problems:

The more time children spend in any of a variety of non-maternal care arrangements across the first 4.5 years of life, the more externalizing problems and conflict with adults they manifest at 54 months of age and in kindergarten, as reported by mothers, caregivers, and teachers.... more time

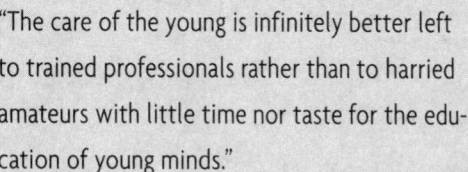

What a Feminist Icon Said:

"The care of the young is infinitely better left to trained professionals rather than to harried amateurs with little time nor taste for the education of young minds."

—Kate Millet,
Feminist author

in care not only predicts problem behavior measured on a continuous scale but at-risk (though not clinical) levels of problem behavior, as well as assertiveness, disobedience, and aggression. It should also be noted that these correlational findings also imply that lower levels of problems were associated with less time in child care.[21]

In addition to the evidence on daycare's links to behavioral disorders and other emotional problems, some researchers have suggested that increased use of daycare—more specifically, the relative absence of mothers in their children's live—may have contributed to disturbing social trends. In *Home-Alone America: The Hidden Toll of Day Care, Behavioral Drugs, and Other Parent Substitutes*, Mary Eberstadt argues that there could be a link between the increase in maternal absence and growth of social pathologies in American children and teenagers, such as mental problems, behavioral problems, and sexually transmitted diseases.[22]

Clearly, there are numerous explanations for all of these problems other than the increasing number of working moms. But Eberstadt makes a compelling case that there's cause for concern and that maternal absence could be a contributing factor. Based on the strong, if only circumstantial, evidence, the link merits more research. After all, this social trend could have serious effects on our nation's children—something we can't just ignore in the name of political correctness.

Eberstadt also casts a new perspective on the debate when she turns the focus away from questions about the long term affects of daycare on children and instead focuses on the experience of young children who are placed in daycare. She highlights how chil-

A Book You're Not Supposed to Read

Day Care Deception: What the Child Care Establishment Isn't Telling Us, Brian C. Robertson; San Francisco, Encounter Books, 2003.

dren in daycare centers tend to experience much higher incidents of illness than their counterparts raised at home. For example, an American Academy of Pediatrics fact sheet, "Controlling Illness in Child Care Programs," lists ailments commonly spread in daycare, from the common cold to gastrointestinal problems to any number of skin and eye infections (impetigo, lice, ringworm, scabies, cold sores, and conjunctivitis, or pinkeye).[23]

Researchers debate the long-term affects of the increased incidence of illness on children. Some believe that the increased exposure has physical benefits for kids, in terms of making them more resistant to ailments later in life. But Eberstandt urges consideration of the actual experience of the child facing the additional physical discomfort of illness during his first years of life: "Shouldn't his unhappiness and confusion and lack of fulfillment count for something in the day care calculus, too?"[24]

Making the decision to work

We all know that children of mothers who work full-time can thrive. The negative research on daycare doesn't mean that women need to quit their jobs and return home. There are notable benefits to having mom in the workforce, such as a higher household income, but those benefits need to be weighed against the potential downsides of daycare.

Parents need to be aware of existing research as they weigh whether and how much to work. Awareness of these issues may encourage some mothers to take different jobs that allow more time at home, even if they provide lower pay. For other women, awareness of these issues won't change their decisions to work, but may make them more vigilant about looking for warning signs in their children for problem behaviors.

Chapter Fourteen

POLITICS: ALL WOMEN DON'T THINK ALIKE

*E*ach election season, political pundits discuss the "women's vote"—the implication being that women vote in mass. The media regularly calls on groups like the NOW to represent "women's" opinions. But NOW doesn't represent women—it represents a subset of women on the Left.

Women are politically divided, splitting nearly evenly between Democrats and Republicans in the 2004 election. Women also don't vote based on so-called "women's issues"; they are primarily concerned about security and the economy, just like men.

Women also aren't automatic supporters of female candidates—any candidate has to earn women's votes, and that's how it should be.

Women's political power

1992 was dubbed "the year of the woman" by the mainstream media, due to the historic election of twenty-four new women to the House of Representatives, five to the Senate, and a swell of women voters. While 1992 may be popular cultures' official "year of the woman," news stories regularly speculate about the next "year of the woman," or how women will once again wield such political prowess at the ballot box. There is no

Guess what?

- Women don't vote as a monolithic block in America.

- The feminist assumption is that women care about different issues than men. But polling data collected during the 2004 election showed that women's top voting priorities were remarkably similar to men's.

- Contrary to what most feminist groups suggest, abortion was not a top consideration of most women voters.

"year of the man"—except perhaps 1994, when the mainstream media decided it was "angry white males" who threw the equivalent of an electoral tantrum by voting in Republican majorities to the House and the Senate.

Part of women's fabled political power undoubtedly stems from the politically correct media, which was thrilled with the results of the "year of the woman" in 1992 and was equally aghast by the results in 1994. The dominant media outlets perpetuate the notion of the next year of the woman in hopes that women will help sweep their fellow liberals back into power.

American women, indisputably, wield great political power—even though a woman has yet to be president (or even run for president on a major party's ticket) and women constitute just 15 percent of Members of Congress.[1] According to CNN's exit polls, women accounted for 54 percent of all votes in the last presidential election. Women were nearly evenly divided between the two candidates—with 48 percent voting for President George W. Bush and 51 percent supporting the democratic nominee, Senator John F. Kerry.

It isn't just women's numbers that make them particularly influential. Women remain "undecided" voters for longer and are more open than men to supporting different candidates. Therefore women are considered "swing voters," or voters who can be swayed by a candidate. As a result, many political messages are targeted directly at women.

Gallup's tracking poll during the run up to the 2004 presidential election showed that while men's support varied, men were relatively consistent in giving President Bush between a five and fifteen percentage point edge. Women's support fluctuated much more wildly. Senator Kerry at one point in the campaign enjoyed a seventeen percentage point advantage among women, but just two months later, women gave President Bush a double digit lead.

What's the gender gap?

The gender gap refers to the difference in voting preferences between men and women; in recent decades, the gender gap is the result of women favoring the Democratic candidate and men favoring the Republican candidate.

The gender gap became more prominent—and widely discussed—during the 1980s after President Reagan's election, when women were much less enthusiastic in their support for Reagan than were men. Before that election, men and women's voting preferences were very similar; and prior to 1964, women were more likely to favor Republican candidates than were men. The gender gap shrunk during the election of George H.W. Bush and again with the first election of President Clinton, but reemerged in 1996 and ballooned during the 2000 election.

According to CNN exit polls, the gender gap shrunk considerably between 2000 and 2004, since women were nearly evenly split between President Bush and Senator Kerry. Women gave Kerry just a three percentage point edge, while men gave President Bush an eleven percentage point edge. Therefore, the total gender gap was fourteen percentage points. In 2000, the gender gap was even more pronounced since men still gave Bush an eleven point edge, but women also gave Vice President Al Gore an eleven point edge so the total gender gap was twenty-two percentage points.

When political pundits talk about the "gender gap," they typically are referring to women's preference for Democratic candidates. Men's pro-Republican tendencies are seldom covered. As Ellen R.

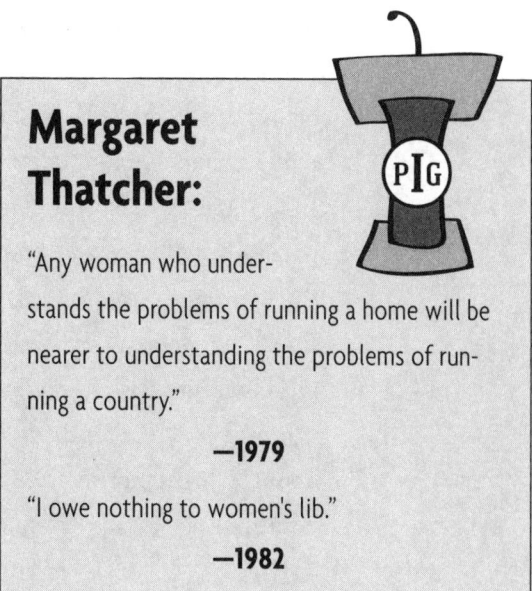

Margaret Thatcher:

"Any woman who understands the problems of running a home will be nearer to understanding the problems of running a country."

—1979

"I owe nothing to women's lib."

—1982

Malcolm, president of Emily's List, a liberal activist groups that supports the election of pro-choice female candidates, insisted in an editorial before the 2004 election:

> The gender gap, a factor in every presidential election since 1980, reflects the difference in the voting patterns of men and women. Though the gap has fluctuated over time, its meaning has been consistent. On the issues that women care about—education, health care, job creation, and the economy—women trust Democrats more than Republicans to fight for their priorities.[2]

True enough. But that analysis overlooks the reality that men are equally fervent—and in the 2004 election were more so—in their belief that the Republican candidates better protected *their* interests.

Women's priorities

When political strategists talk about appealing to women, they often refer to "women's issues." These typically are seen as issues that directly affect women and their families: abortion, childcare, education, workplace discrimination, and healthcare. President Clinton was seen as a master at using these "kitchen table issues" to his advantage.

In the 2004 election, female strategists complained that Senator Kerry wasn't doing enough to talk about "women's issues." One article late in the campaign stated: "It wasn't until well into the presidential debates that Kerry began reaching out to women. Finally, to the satisfaction of women's groups, Kerry firmly established himself as pro-choice and pledged to do something about the wage gap that has women earning about 72 cents for every $1 a man makes." Gloria Steinem echoed these complaints: "He's at the mercy of consultants who are worried about the white male vote . . . so he talks about hunting and military leadership. In the process, the majority of women's issues are neglected."[3]

The feminist assumption is that women care about different issues than men. But polling data collected during the election told a different story: Women's top voting priorities were remarkably similar to men's. Women were most concerned about security issues, the situation in Iraq, and the U.S. economy.

A Gallup poll conducted on October 22 to 24 revealed that the economy was the most frequently cited issue for women who were asked their top priority for voting for president. But the situation in Iraq (26 percent) and potential for terrorism (25 percent) together were the top priorities of a majority of women. This poll mirrored numerous polls taken around the election and suggests that men and women had similar concerns when deciding on a president.

Contrary to what most feminist groups claim, abortion was not a top consideration of most women voters. In a *Marie Claire* poll taken before the 2004 election, only 9 percent responded that abortion would matter in determining their vote, and those who said abortion would matter were twice as likely to be pro-life as pro-choice.

Women support candidates they believe in, not other women

The American public increasingly is comfortable with the idea of having a woman president. Gallup has been asking the question "would you vote for a woman candidate" for president since 1937. And while there have been times in our history when less than half of Americans would vote for a female candidate, today, nearly nine in ten voters say they would consider voting a woman into the Oval Office.

In the latest Gallup poll, men and women were willing almost equally to consider voting for a female president. Eighty-five percent of men and 89 percent of women said they were open to a female president.

However, it's difficult to isolate the affect of gender, because of political beliefs and ideology. As discussed, men are more likely to support Republican candidates while women are more likely to support Democrats. When asked to think about voting for a woman for president in May 2003, many men and women likely thought of Hillary Clinton, since she is by far the most frequently mentioned female candidate for the office. Many men—particularly conservative men—may have thought specifically about her when they say they would not consider voting for a woman for president.

Research conducted by two professors suggests that Democrats are more likely to vote for women:

> Democrats and Independents are consistently less likely to believe the Republican candidate (regardless of the candidate's gender) "shares my concerns," "is qualified," "can be trusted," or "is a strong leader" than Republicans. Republican candidates begin with a big disadvantage, among Democrats and Independents. . . . the Republican female candidate can make up for some of the skepticism engendered by their Republicanism because of being female.[4]

It's impossible to know if this additional support is based on a desire for more women to be in office or greater trust in the personal character of a woman; or if it stems from an assumption that the female Republican candidate will be more liberal and therefore more appealing to Democrat and independent voters than the average Republican.

Similarly, in 2002, pollsters highlighted the important role that party affiliation plays along with gender. While the research revealed that Democratic female candidates tend to get more support from women—

even more than Democratic male candidates receive—they hesitated to attribute this solely to gender affinity. They noted that "Democratic women have usually included women's issues in their campaigns." In other words, it may be the issues that are attracting women, not feelings of sisterhood.[5]

Some evidence suggests that Republicans asked to participate in these opinion surveys also may assume that the women candidate is less conservative than a male candidate. One study found that those who identified themselves as "strong" Republicans were significantly less likely to vote for a generic female candidate than a generic male candidate. But the study also indicated that the strong Republican assumed that the female candidate was less conservative than the male, a perception fueled by a media that consistently showcases liberal feminist organizations as the official spokeswomen for all women.[6] In other words, once again, its ideology and issues that are at the foundation of the decision of who to support, not sexism.

Political pundits anticipating a surge of support from women voters for a female candidate are likely to be disappointed. As one researcher concluded: "Voters are not automatically drawn to candidates simply because they are of the same sex; party and political position are of greater concern when choosing a candidate to vote for."[7]

Conclusion

Women don't vote as a monolithic block in America. They may skew more liberal than American men, but they're more politically diverse than the mainstream media report.

Women need to look beyond the mainstream media to get information about politics and policy since the media often shares the sympathies of the liberal feminist groups and candidates. As will be discussed in the next chapter, that agenda has significant pitfalls for women.

Chapter Fifteen

DIVORCING UNCLE SAM

nfettered abortion rights may be the centerpiece of the feminist agenda, but the feminist movement also has a robust economic agenda. This agenda would expand the size and scope of the federal government and create incentives for women to conform to the feminist vision of what they think women *should* want.

This final chapter is an overview of some key policy issues. It provides a vision of government quite different from what's espoused in women's studies programs, women's magazines, and feminist organizations. It dissects the positions taken by most feminist organizations and makes the case that these positions are inconsistent with women's independence. In fact, many have exactly the opposite effect and are creating a group of women dependent on the government.

The slanted perspective given to women

American women may be politically divided, but so-called representatives of the women's vote tend to speak with one voice. Groups like NOW, National Women's Law Center, Feminist Majority, and Emily's List (among the most prominent women's organizations in the country) have a common agenda. They want a larger government that's more involved

Guess what?

- Feminist groups want a larger government and overwhelmingly support liberal Democrats during elections.

- Today's feminists want women freed from having to rely on husbands or family for support. They pine for a new protector: Uncle Sam.

- Dependence on government is not independence.

in redistributing wealth and providing more services for its citizens. They overwhelmingly support liberal Democrats during elections.

This political agenda is echoed in women's studies centers and courses throughout the country. Often the biases aren't veiled—they're openly declared and fiercely partisan. Consider this passage from the preface of the textbook, *Issues in Feminism: An Introduction to Women's Studies*:

> The 1990s have given us The Contract on America, the virulent racism and misogyny of the religious and political right, attacks against the poorest and must vulnerable among us—welfare mothers and children—and a deepening backlash that is reflected in a spectrum of elements so bizarre they take one's breath away—from the anti-woman pseudofeminists, to patriarchy-worshipping "Promise Keepers," to social "scientists" suddenly discovering and suddenly becoming concerned about absent fathers and negative (or nonexistent) role models.[1]

This same section refers to Republicans as "overtly opposed not only to women's rights but to advances in civil rights in general."[2]

The author goes on to detail explicitly women's studies unique role in activating students to enter the political fight—and to fight for a specific agenda: "Women's studies is faced with a vast responsibility.... We must prepare the present generation for its participation in the women's struggle, but we must do so in an era of hardening antagonism and diminishing resources."[3]

Clearly, women's studies isn't a typical academic discipline. In most fields, college classrooms are a forum in which professors present students with information and interpretations, ask them to consider a variety of view points, and encourage them to draw their own conclusions. Women's studies is proud to thwart these norms and "consciously rejects many traditional forms of inquiry, concepts, and explanatory systems; at the same time, it is developing new and sometimes unique traditions and authorities of its own."[4] In a "feminist classroom," one is likely to find some alternative projects and methods of evaluation, including "credit for social change activities or life experience, contracts of self-grading, diaries and journals, even meditation or ritual."[5]

Women's studies' leaders recognize that some students will recoil at these unusual teaching methods, and warn of the potential for "classroom harassment" in a section entitled, "resistance to women's studies." What kind of behavior do teachers have to be prepared to confront? The list of offending behavior includes "challenging facts with particularist anecdotes to undermine the credibility of feminist reading materials and instructors."[6]

It's a heavy burden for a teacher to be asked factual questions. This aversion to students questioning facts is particularly interesting given the numerous critiques that have revealed how women's studies classes often have a loose definition of "fact." Women's studies programs are notorious for misusing statistics and repeating misleading information on topics ranging from rape and domestic violence to the prevalence of eating disorders and the size of the wage gap.[7]

The rejection of academic rigor suggests that women's studies programs have another purpose. It's not simply a field of study for college students—an alternative to English literature, history, or politics. Women's studies is a recruitment device for a political movement. As Shelia Ruth details in her women's studies 101 textbook, "Today, as in the past, if we lose our rootedness in the women's movement, in concrete social action, we will lose not only our passion but our heart, our meaning, and our whole point."[8]

Selling more than fashion and make-up tips

Women's magazines aren't nearly as overt in pushing a political or policy agenda on their readers as women's studies professors, but they almost always slant to the Left.

Glamour magazine, for example, delved into the world of policy in its June 2005 issue, with a discussion of potential reforms to the Social Security system. They warned readers that the topic may sound like a "yawn," but it's terribly important to women. Yet the article's substance did little to inform readers of the facts about Social Security's financial crisis and the need for reform. It merely echoed liberal attacks on proposed changes and quoted three "non-partisan" representatives, all of whom came from notoriously leftist women's groups.

Similarly, the April 2004 *Ladies' Home Journal* contained an article titled "Armed and Dangerous." The teaser for the piece states: "The battle over gun control rages on as lethal weapons become easier, and cheaper, to buy. Are you and your family safe?" The clear answer to the article, which contains stories of a gun accidentally firing and paralyzing a child, the death of a police officer, and terrorists attempting to exploit the "gun show loophole" to obtain weapons, is "no"—your family isn't safe but more laws will make it safe.

Little discussion is given to the arguments of those on the other side of the gun control debate, such as evidence of how guns are used by law abiding citizens to prevent crime or the failure of existing laws to prevent the arming of criminals. *Ladies' Home Journal* could have told the story of a Florida woman, whose home was broken into but who was able to find her gun in the dark and defend herself by shooting the intruder.[9] Indeed, there are numerous examples of women who lawfully use guns in self-defense to keep from being victims of violent crime. This article instead closes with a call to readers to visit the website of the liberal antigun group, the Brady Campaign to Prevent Gun Violence, to find out more on the issue.

Such slanted coverage of political issues is also typical of morning and daytime television talk shows—such as *Good Morning America*, *Today*, and *Oprah*—which echo the agenda of liberal women's groups on issues

Indoctrination: Women's Studies

*T*he National Women's Studies Association's original constitution, written in 1982, highlighted the link between women's studies and the feminist movement:

Because

⊕ Feminist education is a process deeply rooted in the women's movement and remains accountable to that community.

⊕ Feminist aims include the elimination of oppression and discrimination on the basis of sex, race, age, class, religion, ethnicity, and sexual orientation, as well as other barriers to human liberation inherent in the structure of our society;

⊕ Feminist education is not only the pursuit of knowledge about women, but also the development of knowledge for women, a force which furthers the realization of feminist aims;

Therefore

⊕ The National Women's Studies Association actively supports and promotes feminist education and supports the persons involved in that effort, at any educational level and in any educational setting.[13]

like gun control, the environment, and greater government regulation and spending for innumerable programs.

The Media Research Center regularly documents the liberal bias of these shows, such as when Katie Couric interviewed a nine-year-old, Noah McCullough, famous for his political trivia expertise, about his support for President Bush's plan to reform Social Security. Couric not only challenged him about the policy; she asked his mother if she worried he was "being exploited for political reasons" since the group he worked with had spent millions supporting the president. Did she have difficulty seeing "eye to eye" with her son on the issues, Couric also asked? Her assumption was that this woman couldn't actually agree with her son's positions.

In another incident, during a segment in February 2005, Couric extolled the virtues of the feminism movement, repeating the claim that women make 79 cents for every man's dollar, and never offered viewers a conservative or dissenting opinion.

The feminist philosophy of government

Given that college classrooms and mainstream media tends to echo the agenda of the feminist Left, it's important to examine their policy agenda. The feminist movement largely has come full circle on this front, abandoning the legacy of the early feminists, who championed the belief that women deserve the same rights as men. Those pioneering women fought the idea that women are incapable of taking care of themselves and need the protection of a husband or father. They challenged society to give women more access and opportunity to participate in the public realms of business and politics.

Today's feminists have a very different agenda. While they still want women freed from having to rely on husbands or family for support, they no longer want women to make it on their own merits and hard work. They pine for a new protector: Uncle Sam.

Feminists envision a vastly expanded federal government that collects more taxes, provides more benefits—including subsidizing healthcare, daycare, and welfare programs—and administers a more robust thicket of regulations that dictate what people and businesses can and cannot do. In supporting this big government agenda, feminist groups often make explicitly paternalistic statements, suggesting that women require government to watch over them—reinforcing the harmful notion that women are incapable of surviving or prospering on their own.

Dependence on government is not independence. Women should consider some of the consequences of the feminist big government agenda, which would give politicians and bureaucrats greater control of our lives.

By contrast, policies that return control to individuals have the potential to make women more independent and better off.

Taxation

Feminist organizations regularly oppose reductions in tax rates. Their rhetoric implies that there's no tax too high for women to bear, and that women should prefer government to spend money on their behalf rather than having to make choices on their own.

In many ways, taxes are a necessary evil. The government was established to perform certain tasks that would be difficult if not impossible for individuals or communities to accomplish on their own. This includes maintaining a legal system, protecting individual rights, and defending our country against foreign threats. To perform these vital services, the government needs money and the most efficient way to raise that money is by taxing citizens.

But it's in the nation's best interest to keep those taxes as low as possible (unfortunately, today, the average working American loses one-third of his or her income to government each year). When you think about taxes, the real question to ask yourself is "who is going to put that money to better use—the individuals who earned it or the politicians in Washington, D.C.?" One need only look at the federal government's budget—loaded with ludicrous spending projects that help a few favored constituents or special causes—to see why it's preferable to keep taxes low and the federal government lean.

Everyone knows that the government is wasteful. Yet even when it spends money on what sounds like good ideas, it often ends up crowding out private initiatives and affecting individual behavior.

Take the example of government investment in new technologies. It may seem sensible for government to invest in the creation of new technologies, because we all recognize that technology plays an important role in our quality of life. But when government invests in new technologies, it tilts the playing field toward certain technologies and companies and away from others. But the bureaucrats picking projects to fund know less than millions of individual investors, so inevitably some inventions will take up resources that could be used better elsewhere. Companies also start focusing on how to please the government and politicians, instead of how to make things that will be most useful to consumers, and therefore, best rewarded in the marketplace.

America leads the world in high-tech innovation because our private market allows individuals and businesses to invest in promising technologies. Those investors, motivated by profit, are diligent in selecting companies that are most likely to be successful producing the best products. Government intervention into this market takes resources from the private sector leaving investors with less money to invest and forcing them to take into account how government is going to pick winners and losers.

The collection of taxes also impacts the choices consumers and workers make. Consider the situation faced by a married woman who has been out of the workforce caring for her children, but is considering getting a formal job. The money she earns is going to be added on to her husband's income so she'll typically face a very high marginal tax rate. After paying payroll taxes, income taxes, and state and local taxes, this married woman is likely to take home less than half of the money she earns. The rest is soaked up by the government. She may very well decide that it isn't worth it for her to take the job.

At the same time, high taxes make it difficult for some families to afford to keep a parent at home. Since government takes such a large portion of income, the money earned by just one spouse may not be enough to make ends meet. As a result, many women who would prefer to be at home raising their children have to enter the workforce to increase the family's after-tax income.

The negative reactions of traditional feminist groups to policies that would return resources to wage-earners reinforces an antiquated notion of women as wards of the state. But women aren't just consumers of social services; they are also taxpayers. Women, like men, would benefit from lower tax rates that give individuals—not Washington—control over their money.

Social Security

America's Social Security system was created in 1935. Today, it faces serious financial challenges. In just ten years, Social Security will begin running a deficit—it will take in less through payroll taxes than it needs to pay out in benefits. By 2041, when today's thirty-year-olds are getting ready to retire, Social Security will be bankrupt and taking in only enough revenue to pay about 70 percent of promised benefits.

The root of Social Security's problem is its system of financing. Social Security uses what is called "pay-as-you-go" financing, which is really another term for tax-and-spend. Workers currently lose 12.4 percent of their income to Social Security taxes, which is used to pay benefits to current retirees; nothing is saved for their own future retirement. This system may have been adequate in 1950, when sixteen workers were paying into Social Security for each retiree, but today just over three workers support each person collecting checks. By 2050, only two workers will be paying for each retiree's Social Security. This means that, if nothing is done, future workers will either see their taxes soar to pay for Social Security or future retirees will see their benefits slashed.

Raising taxes or cutting benefits to make Social Security's accounts balance would make the system's other major flaw—that it's a terrible deal for young workers—even worse. Under current law, many young workers can expect to get a negative rate of return on the money they put into

Social Security, which means they would have been better off putting their money under their mattress.

Policymakers need to find a way to address both of these problems, by putting Social Security on the road to long-term solvency and giving workers the chance to earn a better rate of return on their money. The best way to do so is by allowing young workers to use a portion of the money that they already pay into Social Security to fund a personal retirement account, much like a 401(k), which can be invested in stocks and bonds. This would give workers the chance to enjoy the higher rate of return that comes from investing in real assets. It would also begin to fund future benefits, an important step toward financial stability. Instead of relying solely on taxes from future workers to pay future benefits, retirees would draw upon assets built up over prior decades.

Personal account plans don't instantly solve all of Social Security's problems. Personal accounts would require an initial infusion of resources and policymakers need to consider additional measures, like common sense benefit adjustments, to make Social Security financial sound. This investment would allow a more financially secure system to emerge—an outcome well worth the initial sacrifice.

Women would particularly benefit from Social Security reform. After all, women live longer and are more likely to depend on Social Security during retirement, so have the most at stake in creating a financial sound system. Women are also less likely than men to work in jobs that have other retirement savings vehicles, which makes it all the more important that the money women are putting away for retirement—their Social Security dollars—is put to the best possible use.

But liberal feminist groups oppose any measures that would give individuals more control over how their payroll taxes are used. Typically these organization attempt to minimize Social Security's financial problems and would prefer to put off making any changes, essentially kicking the problem down the road to the next generation. Not surprisingly, when the feminist groups do offer proposals to address Social Security's financial problems, their rely on raising taxes, which once again result in government expanding and individuals have even less money to spend on their own.

"Free" healthcare

In 1993–1994, Hillary Clinton took a leading role in advocating massive changes to the U.S. healthcare system. Although her proposal was widely criticized and not enacted, how to improve the existing system of healthcare remains an important issue.

American women today live longer and are healthier than at any time in U.S. history. A woman born in 1929 could expect to live to just fifty-nine; a woman born in 2000 can expect a full twenty extra years—living to nearly eighty.

This remarkable increase in longevity is largely attributable to the breakthroughs created within the U.S. healthcare system—a system that is by far the most innovative in the world. The primary driver of American innovation in this field is a market that, while distorted, remains far freer than markets in Europe or Japan. U.S. pharmaceutical and biomedical companies lead the world not because U.S. researchers are inherently smarter, but because they have a profit-motive to develop and deliver new treatments and cures.

Feminist groups view the profit motive with suspicion and would prefer to put government in charge of our nation's healthcare system. Once again, they favor government control rather than leaving decisions up to individuals. They look admiringly at systems in Europe and Canada where governments dictate access to healthcare services, echoing the principles that Hillary Clinton articulated in the 1990s.

Advocates of nationalized healthcare focus on benefits such as more access for the low-income population to preventative care, but overlook the drawbacks to the single-payer healthcare system, including reduced innovation and the rationing of care. Canadians wait an average of 7.3 weeks to see a specialist after their family doctor makes a referral under Canada's celebrated single payer, healthcare system. They wait another 9.2 weeks between seeing the specialist and receiving treatment.[10] For women, the median wait between a referral by a general practitioner and an appointment with a specialist in gynecology was eight weeks in 2004; the wait between meeting the specialist and treatment was nearly seven weeks.[11]

Instead of pushing policies that would give government more control over our healthcare system, policymakers should consider ways to put power back in the hands of patients. One of the most promising reforms is Health Savings Accounts (HSAs). HSAs allow individuals to put a portion of their pre-tax money into an investment account which can then be used to purchase healthcare services. An individual with an HSA must have a high-deductible health plan, but can use the money in the account to pay the cost of initial medical expenses. Unused balances in the account are invested and accumulate for future use.

Essentially, HSAs turn individuals into true healthcare consumers, with an incentive to make prudent healthcare choices, seek lower prices, and use only the services they need. It forces healthcare providers to consider how to attract patients and address their unique needs, since those patients are customers who can take their business elsewhere.

Women should consider the benefits of a healthcare system that puts more control in the hands of individuals and the pitfalls of the feminist recipe of giving more power to government.

Women and work

Feminist organizations push policies designed to make the working world more accessible to women, particularly, mothers. The underlying purpose is to make their vision of what women should want—full-time jobs and kids in daycare—into reality. These policies ignore the real desires of many individual women and have unintended consequences that make it more difficult for women to find work arrangements most suited to their needs.

As discussed in chapter thirteen, government-funded daycare is a favorite of groups like NOW. Yet while the government can make daycare seem "free" to working parents, it isn't free to taxpayers. Passing on those costs means families who have one spouse at home will have a tougher time making ends meet. Stay-at-home-moms' service would be devalued since they could be replaced by the "free" substitute: government day-care centers. This proposal would push stay-at-home moms to seek for-mal employment.

Instead of finding ways to make institutional care more affordable for parents, policymakers ought to consider leveling the playing field to make it easier for parents to stay home with their children. Not only does research suggest that having more parents at home may be better for chil-dren, but it's also the daycare arrangement that most men and women say that they would prefer.

The Public Agenda survey confirmed this preference. Parents sup-ported policies that would "make it easier and more affordable for one parent to stay at home" over policies that that would "improve the cost and quality of child care" by a margin of 62 percent to 30 percent. This stands in stark contrast to the opinions of the so-called "children's advo-cates," seven out of ten of whom wanted public policy to move in the direction of a universal child care system.

Some feminist organizations and left-leaning politicians lambaste attempts to make life easier and more affordable for stay-at-home parents as "giveaways to the rich," but the evidence simply doesn't support this characterization. The highest number of stay-at-home moms comes from families earning between $20,000 and $25,000—hardly what we consider rich in the United States. Policies that subsidize center-based care often end up transferring resources from a less financially well-off group (families with a single earner) to a richer demographic (dual-earning couples).[12]

Policymakers should listen to parents, not the rhetoric of organizations or experts who claim to speak on behalf of women and children. Instead of focusing on making daycare more affordable, policymakers should consider how to make it easier for parents to adopt their ideal daycare arrangement—which, more often than not, is having one parent stay home.

Government should also steer clear of mandates that purport to make it easier for women to balance family and work, such as requiring employers to offer benefits of lengthy periods of leave. Such policies have good intentions, but can limit women's employment options and reduce their salaries. According to Massachusetts Institute of Technology economist Jonathan Gruber, the real wages of married women in states with laws mandating comprehensive coverage for maternity expenses fell, while wages rose in states without the mandate on business. In other words, the costs of the mandates were passed on to the intended beneficiaries. Gruber's research provides evidence for what most people instinctively understand: Policies that force an employer to spend more on particular workers make those workers less attractive financially and reduces their take home pay.

They can also limit the availability of employment. Government demands that businesses provide health insurance or leave benefits to their employees create an incentive for businesses to hire fewer workers. The consequences of the regulations are more pronounced for women who move in and out of the workforce and are more likely to seek part-time employment or other nontraditional work relationships.

Occasionally, feminists promote policies designed specifically to benefit stay-at-home moms, whose work, they argue, is "uncompensated" since women don't receive a paycheck for their services. Naomi Wolf and

Danielle Crittenden, for example, want stay-at-home moms to receive a "Social Security credit" for their work, even though they pay no payroll taxes.

This attempted to institute government policies to reward the stay-at-home mom is just as misguided as their policies to favor working moms. The government would have to "assign" a value to the work of the stay-at-home mom, which would likely start a political bidding war. Consider how unfair it is to a mother who is working and desperately wishes to stay home but she can't afford it. Let's assume that the government decides to credit the stay-at-home mom the national average wage for Social Security purposes. The working woman loses more than one dollar in Social Security taxes in every ten dollars she earns. If she earns the same as a stay-at-home mom's government-mandated wage, she'd be paying thousands of dollars in taxes for the same Social Security benefit.

Instead of pushing programs that favor a particular lifestyle, government should focus on facilitating flexibility for everyone. Lowering taxes and reducing government spending, for example, would reduce the fiscal burden on all families—without favoring one choice over another. Families with a parent at home could stretch one income further, and working women would have larger incomes to

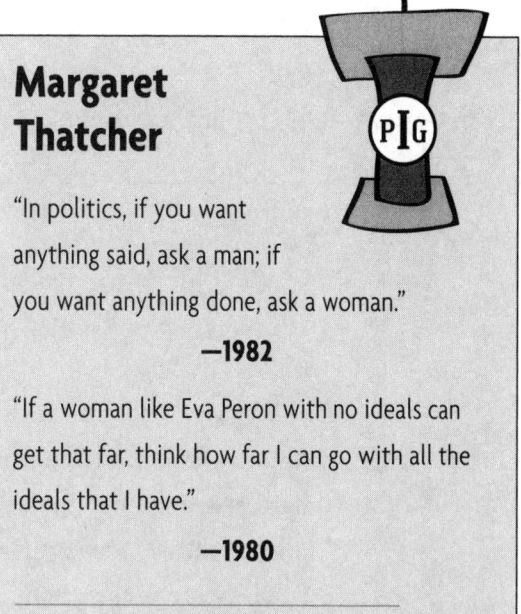

Margaret Thatcher

"In politics, if you want anything said, ask a man; if you want anything done, ask a woman."

—1982

"If a woman like Eva Peron with no ideals can get that far, think how far I can go with all the ideals that I have."

—1980

http://news.bbc.co.uk/1/hi/uk_politics/1888444.stm (all Thatcher quotes use this link)

purchase child care. Paring back costly regulations would allow businesses to hire new employees and offer more flexible work arrangements—something that may appeal both to women already working and

What a Feminist Icon Said:

"There is not the woman born who desires to eat the bread of dependence, no matter whether it be from the hand of father, husband, or brother; for any one who does so eat her bread places herself in the power of the person from whom she takes it."

—Susan B. Anthony

http://quotations.about.com/cs/morepeople/a/Susan_B_Anthony_2.htm

to some homebound moms who may enjoy part-time jobs.

Government can't erase the challenges that women face in trying to balance work and family. The best government can do is to remain neutral and let women make decisions based on their own preferences.

Affirmative action

Feminist calls for affirmative action are the most explicit example of their belief that women are less capable than men and in need of special consideration. Proponents argue that women should receive favored treatment in employment and in education to overcome the pervasive sexism that holds women back. But the message is that left on their own, women are less likely to succeed than men and need the bar lowered for them.

Whether affirmative action policies actually lower standards and reward less qualified individuals, they certainly suggest that a lower standard is used, creating the perception of undeserved reward and tarnishing the earned accomplishments of the policy's intended beneficiaries.

There are times when it is useful to compensate for differences in ability or experience. Golf courses are designed to let women and men compete against each other more evenly. "Ladies' tees" take into account the biological fact that, in general, women have less physical strength than do men, and therefore are not going to be able to drive the ball as far down the course.

Ladies' tees make sense since it's generally accepted that biological differences give men an advantage in the game of golf. However, women should be concerned by policies that attempt to set up "ladies' tees" in other areas of life—like education and employment. Policies that favor women on criteria such as intellect and initiative demean the accomplishments of successful women. Affirmative action creates an environment in which people wonder if these women truly earned their success or if they merely rose to the top of a rigged game.

Sexism does exist. Women will probably always face gender-related challenges—but they will have to clear those hurdles one at a time. Embracing affirmative action institutionalizes a far more damaging form of sexism: the official recognition of an assumption of female inferiority. Feminist groups make a grievous error when they pursue government-mandated advantages; true feminism means trusting that women can compete and succeed on their own.

School choice

Feminist groups often hold themselves up as champions of "choice." But it turns out this rhetoric applies solely to a woman's choice of whether or not to carry a child to term. When it comes to some of the most important decisions about raising that child, they want to limit choice and keep the government firmly in charge.

Consider feminists' hostility to school choice proposals. For more than a decade, school choice has flourished: Policymakers across the country have been embracing proposals—from charter schools and public school choice to vouchers and education tax credits—that give parents greater ability to select a school for their child. Fifteen years ago, there was no such thing as a charter school. Today, about 2,695 charter schools serve 685,000 students. In spite of fierce opposition from teacher's unions, voucher programs, including the program in Washington D.C., are help-ing give low-income parents the option to choose a private school for their children.

This momentum is fueled by a growing body of research, which sug-gests that competition in education works. Competition leads to greater parental satisfaction and better student performance and behavior, including higher test scores. Educational systems faced with competition use their resources more wisely, leading to improvements for kids who opt for a new school as well as those students who remain in the public school system.

Unfortunately, groups that typically claim to speak for women—such as NOW and American Association of University Women—have ignored this evidence and continue to defend the status quo. They support the calls of the education lobby for more money, despite a lack of evidence that money alone solves any problems.

Feminists' failure to support school choice proposals has conse-quences beyond the classroom. Women and families are affected directly by school choice and the lack there of. After all, there is one form of school choice that currently exists everywhere in America—location-based school choice. Families can move and enroll in another public school.

That option is available only to those who have the means to move. Many families make significant financial sacrifices to buy a house in a superior school district. Some women may work just to afford to live in this district, but would prefer to stay home. School choice programs, by giving parents a new method of choosing a school, could ease the finan-cial pressure that drives these women into the work place.

There are many reasons to embrace school choice proposals, from the potential benefits for children's education to the increased flexibility for mothers and fathers. Feminists should also listen to their own rhetoric: parents should have more choice when it comes to their children.

Get More Information on All of These Issues

Find out more about how these and other important policy issues affect women:

The Independent Women's Forum, *www.iwf.org*
American Enterprise Institute, *www.aei.org*
Atlas Economic Research Foundation, *www.atlasusa.org*
The Cato Institute. *www.cato.org*
Citizens Against Government Waste, *www.cagw.org*
The Competitive Enterprise Institute, *www.cei.org*
The Goldwater Institute, *www.goldwaterinstitute.org*
The Heritage Foundation, *www.heritage.org*
National Center for Policy Analysis, *www.ncpa.org*
Manhattan Institute for Policy Research, *www.manhattan-institute.org*
State Policy Network, *www.spa.org*

An agenda for women

Instead of following the feminist lead of constantly pushing for bigger government, women should embrace an agenda of returning power to individuals and limiting the size and scope of government. This agenda would include lowering taxes, reforming Social Security, education, and healthcare to give individuals more control of their resources, and reducing regulations.

Women are capable of competing and succeeding on their own merits. With government out of the way and women empowered to make decisions in the interests of themselves and their families, America will be better off than ever before.

NOTES

Chapter 1:

The Difference between Boys and Girls

1. Steven E. Rhoads, *Taking Sex Differences Seriously* (San Francisco, Encounter Books, 2004) 16.

2. Ibid., 18.

3. Ibid., 21.

4. Ibid., 22-23.

5. Ibid., 27-28.

6. Ibid., 29.

7. Ibid., 31.

Chapter 2:

Return to Romance

1. Mary Elizabeth Podles, "Tradition and the Sexes," The American Enterprise Online. Available at: http://www.taemag.com/issues/articleid.16204/article_detail.asp.

2. Dr. Warren Farrell, Ph.D, *Why Men Earn More: The Startling Truth Behind the Pay Gap—and What Women Can Do About It*, [New York, AMACOM, 2005] 66-68.

3. Norval D. Glenn and Elizabeth Marquardt, "Hooking Up, Hanging Out and Hoping for Mr. Right: College Women on Dating and Mating Today," Institute for American Values, commission by Independent Women's Forum, July 26, 2001, 5. Available at: http://www.iwf.org/campuscorner/pdf/hookingup.pdf.

4. Ibid., 14.

Chapter 3:

Sex: Love's Got Something to Do with It

1. Doug Thompson, "Sex and the single coed," *Capitol Hill Blue*, October 29, 2002.

2. April Witt, "Blog Interrupted," *Washington Post Magazine*, August 15, 2004, 16.

3. Christina Stolba, "Lying in a Room of One's Own," Independent Women's Forum Special Report, July 1, 2003.

4. Wendy Shalit, *A Return to Modesty: Rediscovering the Lost Virtue*, (Free Press, New York, 2000) 192.

5. Witt, 16.

6. Question 16 in "Questionnaire and Detailed Results: A Series of Surveys on Teens About Sex," The Henry J. Kaiser Family Foundation, October 2003. Available at: www.seventeen.com/sexsmarts.

7. "With One Voice 2003: America's Adults and Teens Sound Off About Teen Pregnancy," National Campaign to Prevent Teen Pregnancy, December 2003, 3. Available at: http://www.teenpregnancy.org/resources/data/pdf/wov2003.pdf.

8. Glenn and Marquardt, 11.

9. Rhoads, 103.

10. Glenn and Marquardt, 14.

11. Alexa Joy Sherman and Nicole Tocandins, *Happy Hook-Up: A Single Girl's Guide to Casual Sex*, (Ten Speed Press, Berkeley, CA, 2004) 27-31.

12. Sherman and Tocandins, 248.

13. Rhoads, 104.

14. Ibid., 107.

15. Ibid., 91.

Chapter 4:

Not Everyone Is Doing It

1. Rhoads, 23.

2. "Virginity and the First Time: A Series of Surveys on Teens About Sex," The Henry J. Kaiser Family Foundation and *Seventeen Magazine*, October 2003. Available at: http://www.seventeen.com/sexsmarts.

3. "Youth Risk Behavior Surveillance—United States, 2003," Morbidity and Mortality Weekly Report, Surveillance Summaries, Department of

Health and Human Services, Centers for Disease Control and Prevention, Vol. 53, No. SS-2, 18. Available at: http://www.cdc.gov/mmwr/PDF/ss/ss5302.pdf.

4. "With One Voice 2003: America's Adults and Teens Sound Off About Teen Pregnancy," 3.

5. "Virginity and the First Time: A Series of Surveys on Teens About Sex."

6. Ibid.

7. "Youth Risk Behavior Surveillance—United States, 2003," 18.

8. "Facts in Brief: Sexual and Reproductive Health: Women and Men," Alan Guttmacher Institute. Available at: http://www.guttmacher.org/pubs/fb_10-02.html.

9. "Virginity and the First Time: A Series of Surveys on Teens About Sex."

10. "With One Voice 2003: America's Adults and Teens Sound Off About Teen Pregnancy," National Campaign to Prevent Teen Pregnancy, December 2003, 2. Available at: http://www.teenpregnancy.org/resources/data/pdf/wov2003.pdf.

Chapter 5:
The Risks of Safe Sex

1. Robert Rector, "The Effectiveness of Abstinence Education Programs in Reducing Sexual Activity Among Youth," Heritage Foundation Backgrounder No. 1533, April 5, 2002.

2. "The Content of Federally Funded Abstinence-Only Education Programs," Prepared for Rep. Henry Waxman, U.S. House of Representatives Committee on Government Reform, Dec. 2004.

3. For example, an intern at the Independent Women's Forum went to a few college campuses in Fall 2004 and found free condoms being distributed by student organizations. For example, on George Washington University's campus, a poster advertised "Join VFC (Voices for Choice) and get free condoms and pro-choice friends."

4. Anastasia Higginbotham, "Chicks Goin' At It," in Barbara Findlen, editor, *Listen Up: Voices from the Next Feminist Generation* (Seal Press, Emeryville, CA, 2001), 17.

5. Jane White, "Are You Ready for Dogging?" *Marie Claire*, May 2005, 103.

6. Ibid., 104.

7. "Factsheet: How is the 34% statistic calculated?" National Campaign to Prevent Teen Pregnancy, Washington, DC, 2004. Available at: http://www.teenpregnancy.org/resources/reading/pdf/35percent.pdf.

8. "Not Just Another Single Issue: Teen Pregnancy Prevention's Link to Other Critical Social Issues," The National Campaign to Prevent Teen Pregnancy, February 2002, 2. Available at: http://www.teenpregnancy.org/resources/data/pdf/notjust.pdf.

9. Ibid.

10. "It's Your (Sex) Life: Your Guide to Safe and Responsible Sex," Henry J. Kaiser Family Foundation, August 18, 2005. Available at: http://www.kff.org/youthhivstds/upload/MTV_Think_IYSL_Booklet.pdf.

11. "Genital Herpes," Health Matters, National Institute for Allergy and Infections Diseases, National Institute of Health, Department of Health and Human Services, September 2003. Available at: http://www.niaid.nih.gov/factsheets/stdherp.htm.

12. "Chlamydia," STD Surveillance 2003, Center for Disease Control, Department of Health and Human Services. Available at: http://www.cdc.gov/std/stats/chlamydia.htm.

13. Rhoads, 108.

14. Ibid.

15. Dr. Meg Meeker, *Epidemic: How Teen Sex Is Killing Our Kids*, (Washington DC, LifeLine Press, 2002) 44.

16. Mary Eberstadt, *Home-Alone America: The Hidden Toll of Day Care, Behavioral Drugs, and Other Parent Substitutes* (New York, Sentinel, 2004) 131.

17. "Workshop Summary: Scientific Evidence of Condom Effectiveness for Sexually Transmitted Disease (STD) Prevention," National Institute of Allergy and Infectious Diseases, National Institutes of Health, Department of Health and Human Services, July 20, 2001, 26.

18. "Male Latex Condoms and Sexually Transmitted Diseases," Fact Sheet for Public Health Personnel, National Center for HIV, STD and TB Prevention, Center for Disease Control, Department of Health and Human Services, available at: http://www.cdc.gov/hiv/pubs/facts/condoms.htm.

19. "Workshop Summary: Scientific Evidence of Condom Effectiveness for Sexually Transmitted Disease (STD) Prevention," 14.

20. Meeker, 99.

21. Ibid., 113.

22. Ibid., 116.

23. Higginbotham, 17.

Chapter 6:
Men Aren't the Enemy

1. Shelia Ruth, *Issues in Feminism: An Introduction to Women's Studies*, Fourth Edition (Mayfield Publishing Company, Mountain View, California, 1998) 256.

2. Higginbotham, 13.

3. *Lifetime* Television. Available at: http://www.lifetimetv.com/community/olc/violence/facts_index.html.

4. Mary F. Rogers and C.D. Garrett, *Who's Afraid of Women's Studies: Feminisms in Everyday Life* (Altamira Press, Walnut Creek, CA, 2002) 42.

5. Margaret L. Anderson, *Thinking About Women: Sociological Perspectives on Sex and Gender*, Fifth Edition (Allyn & Bacon, Needham Heights, MA, 2000) 81.

6. Rogers and Garrett, 45.

7. Ruth, 254.

8. U.S. Department of Justice, Bureau of Justice Statistics, "Homicide Trends in the U.S." available at: http://www.ojp.usdoj.gov/bjs/homicide/gender.htm.

9. Cathy Young, "Domestic Violence: An In-Depth Analysis" Independent Women's Forum, Position Paper No. 504, September 30, 2005.

10. Christina Hoff Sommers, *Who Stole Feminism?: How Women Have Betrayed Women*, (Simon & Schuster, New York, 1995) 188-192.

11. For example, see Ginny Holbert, "Super Bowl Timeout to Protect Women," *Chicago Sun-Times*, January 18, 1993, 30, and "Super Bowl Sunday Leads to Battered Wives, Say Activists," *Orlando Sentinel*, January 30, 1993, A3.

12. Linda J. Waite and Maggie Gallagher, *The Case for Marriage: Why Married People Are Happier, Healthier, and Better Off Financially* (Doubleday, New York, 2000) 150-151.

13. Ibid.

14. Ibid., 154.

15. Ibid., 155.

16. Ibid., 153.

17. Ibid., 155.

18. For example, Gallagher and Waite found that even after controlling for education, race, age, and gender, people who live together are still three times more likely to report violent arguments than married people. Ibid., 156.

19. Callie Marie Rennison, Ph.D and Michael R. Rand, "Criminal Victimization, 2002," Bureau of Justice Statistics National Crime Victimization Survey, August 2003, 3.

20. Sommers, 211.

21. Ibid., 212.

22. Ibid., 214.

Chapter 7:

Marriage: Happier Ever After

1. *Radical Feminism*, edited by Anne Koedt, Ellen Levine, and Anita Rapone, (Quadrangle, New York Times Book Company, 1973) 374.

2. Patrick F. Fagan, Robert E. Rector, and Lauren R. Noyes, "Why Congress Should Ignore Radical Feminist Opposition to Marriage," Heritage Backgrounder #1662, June 16, 2003, 4.

3. Betty Friedan, *The Second Stage* (Summit Books, New York, 1981) 22.

4. Ruth, 235.

5. Ibid.

6. For example, "A husband barters some of his income and freedom for the kind of services and satisfactions a wife provides. What does a wife barter? For the financial security (now not a clear return for the more than 54 percent of all married women who work outside the home), for the status of being married, for love and companionship, women take on almost limitless labors of service to their home and family. Whereas a husband takes on a "job" involving specifiable hours, tasks and rewards, a wife takes on a lifestyle." Ruth, 237. And, "Married women still tend to shoulder most of the care-taking responsibilities in the household; the husband is, among other things, another person within the family needing care. Besides doing domestic labor, a "good" wife is supposed to provide emotional support to the husband. . . . Arlie Hochschild struck a chord in many households when she published her book *The Second Shift*, on the stressful results of this division of labor. Women with children face tremendous burdens when

their marriages break up, but they are also left with one less person to manage." Virginia Sapiro, *Women in American Society: An Introduction to Women's Studies*, Fourth Edition, (Mayfield Publishing Company, Mountain View, California, 1999) 188.

7. Jaclyn Geller, *Here Comes The Bride: Women, Weddings and The Marriage Mystique* (Four Walls Eight Windows, New York, 2001) 71.

8. "The wedding planning magazine FOR YOU," *Philadelphia Tribune*, May 28, 2002, Vol. 118; No. 55; 1B.

9. Waite and Gallagher, 70.

10. Ibid., 67.

11. Ibid., 68.

12. "As American Women See It; Motherhood Today—A Tougher Job, Less Ably Done," The Pew Research Center for People and the Press, May 9, 1997, 5.

13. Ruth, 244-245.

14. Waite and Gallagher, 121. For a longer discussion of the effects of marriage and divorce on women and men's financial security, see 97-123.

15. Elizabeth Warren and Amelia Warren Tyagi, *The Two-Income Trap: Why Middle-Class Mothers & Fathers Are Going Broke* (Basic Books, New York, 2003) 55-70.

16. Waite and Gallagher, 114.

17. Ibid., 113.

18. Charlotte A. Shoenborn, "Marital Status and Health: United States, 1999-2002," Advance Data from Vital and Health Statistics Number 351, U.S. Department of Health and Human Services, Centers for Disease Control and Prevention, National Center for Health Statistics, December 15, 2004, 1. Available at: http://www.cdc.gov/nchs/data/ad/ad351.pdf.

19. Shoenborn, 1.

20. Waite and Gallagher, 47-77.

21. Ibid., 82.

22. Nancy Wartik, "The Perils of Playing House," *Psychology Today*, July/August 2005.

23. Ibid.

24. Ibid.

25. Jennifer Roback Morse, *Smart Sex: Finding Life-Long Love in a Hook-Up World*, (Spence Publishing Company, Dallas, 2005) 50.

26. Ibid., 99.

27. Ibid., 98.

28. E. Kay Trimberger, *The New Single Woman* (Beacon Press, Boston, 2005).

Chapter 8:
Divorce

1. Wendy Murray Zoba, "Take a Little Time Out," ChristianityToday, February 7, 2000. Available at: http://www.christianitytoday.com/ct/2000/002/34.86.html.

2. Barbara Dafoe Whitehead and David Popenoe, "The State of Our Unions: The Social Health of Marriage, 2004" The National Marriage Project, 2004, 15. Available at: http://marriage.rutgers.edu/Publications/SOOU/TEXTSOOU2004.htm.

3. Virginia Sapiro, *Women in American Society: An Introduction to Women's Studies*, Fourth Edition, (Mayfield Publishing Company, Mountain View, California, 1999) 397.

4. Ashton Applewhite, *Cutting Loose: Why Women Who End Their Marriages Do So Well* (HarperCollins Publishers, New York, 1997) xv.

5. Ibid., 2.

6. Ibid., 21.

7. Linda J. Waite, Don Browning, William J. Doherty, Maggie Gallagher, Ye Luo, and Scott M. Stanley, "Does Divorce Make People Happy? Findings from a Study of Unhappy Marriages," Institute for American Values, 2002, 4.

8. Ibid.

9. Ibid., 5.

10. Waite and Gallagher, 149.

11. Waite, Browning, Doherty, Gallagher, Luo, and Stanley, 6.

12. Ibid., 7.

13. Ibid., 7-8.

14. Applewhite, 246.

15. Ibid., 255.

16. Ibid., 249.

17. Waite, Browning, Doherty, Gallagher, Luo, and Stanley, 7.

18. Applewhite, 169-170.

19. Ibid., 171.

20. Patrick F. Fagan, Robert E. Rector, Kirk A. Johnson, Ph.D. and America Peterson "The Positive Effect of Marriage: A Book of Charts," The Heritage Foundation, 30-40. Available at: http://www.heritage.org/Research/Features/Marriage/loader.cfm?url=/commonspot/security/getfile.cfm&PageID=48119.

21. The Positive Effect of Marriage: A Book of Charts, 29. Chart is taken from Cynthia Harper and Sara McLanahan, "Father Absence and Youth Incarceration," paper presented at the annual meeting of the American Sociologoical Association in San Francisco, August 1998. Data from the National Longitudinal Survey of Youth.

22. Judith S. Wallerstein, Julia M. Lewis, and Sandra Blakeslee, *The Unexpected Legacy of Divorce: The 25 Year Landmark Study* (Hyperion, New York, 2000) xxxii-xxxiii.

23. Ibid., 188.

24. Ibid., 90.

25. Ibid., 26.

26. "Contrary to what we have long thought, the major impact of divorce does not occur during childhood or adolescence. Rather, it rises in adulthood as serious romantic relationships move center stage." Ibid., xxxv.

27. Ibid., 299.

28. Ibid., xxxix.

29. Ibid., xxxvii.

30. Ibid., 307.

Chapter 9:
Fertility Facts

1. "Ad plays up biological clock," *Chicago Sun-Times*, August 7, 2001.

2. Betsy Hart, "Delaying Motherhood Ignores Hard Realities," *Chicago Sun-Times*, April 14, 2002.

3. Kim Gandy, "Campaign goes too far," *USA Today*, September 6, 2002, 14A.

4. Michelle Quinn, "Waiting too Long," *San Jose Mercury News*, August 4, 2002.

5. Sapiro, 402-439.

6. Hilary Lips, *Sex & Gender: An Introduction* (Mayfield Publishing Company, Mountain View, California, 1988) 195.

7. Ibid., 196.

8. Arthur Caplan, "Is it ever too late," *The Philadelphia Inquirer*, November 18, 2004, A35.

9. "Patient's Fact Sheet: Prediction of Fertility Potential in Older Female Patients," American Society of Reproductive Medicine, August 1996. Available at: http://www.asrm.org/Patients/FactSheets/Older_Female-Fact.pdf.

10. "Prevention of Infertility Source Document: The Impact of Age on Female Fertility," American Society of Reproductive Medicine, 1. Available at: http://www.protectyourfertility.org/docs/age_femaleinfertility.doc.

11. "Age and Fertility: A Guide for Patients," American Society for Reproductive Medicine, 3. Available at: http://www.asrm.org/Patients/patient-booklets/agefertility.pdf.

12. "Age and Fertility: A Guide for Patients," 6.

13. Richard Scott, MD and Pamela Madsen, "What Mother Didn't Tell You About Fertility...Because No One Ever Told Her," American Infertility Association, 6. Available at: http://www.theafa.org/faqs/afa_whatmother-didnotsay.html.

14. Ibid., 3.

15. Ibid.

16. Psyche Pascual, "Financing Infertility Treatments," "A Healthy Me." Available at: http://www.ahealthyme.com/topic/infertilityfinance.

17. Sylvia Ann Hewlett, *Creating a Life: Professional Women and the Quest for Children* (Talk Miramax Books, New York, 2002) 1.

18. Ibid., 2.

19. Ibid., 3.

20. Ibid., 86

21. Ibid., 86

22. Ibid., 87

23. Frank Newport, "Desire to Have Children Alive and Well in America," The Gallup Poll, August 19, 2003, 2.

24. Hewlett, 9.

Chapter 10:
Abortion

1. "What If *Roe* Fell? The State-by-State Consequences of Overturning *Roe v. Wade*," Center for Reproductive Rights, September 2004.

2. "The Current Situation in the UK," Abortion Rights. Available at: http://www.abortionrights.org.uk/index.php?option=com_content&task=view&id=17&Itemid=44.

3. "Summary of European Abortion Laws," Pregnant Pause. Available at www.pregnantpause.org/lex/lexeuro.htm.

4. Annual Review of Population Law, Available at: http://annualreview.law.harvard.edu/population/abortion/SWEDEN.abo.htm.

5. Steve Doughty, "At 24 weeks, our time limit is most liberal in Europe, *Daily Mail* (London), March 17, 2005.

6. "Abortion Surveillance—United States, 2000," Morbidity and Mortality Week Report, November 28, 2003, Vol. 52, No. SS-12.

7. "Facts in Brief: Induced Abortion," Alan Guttmacher Institute. Available at: www.guttmacher.org/pubs/fb_induced_abortion.html. And, "Fact Sheet: Abortion in the U.S." The Henry J. Kaiser Family Foundation, January 2003.

8. "Induced Abortions," Medical Library, American College of Obstetricians and Gynecologists. Available at: http://www.medem.com/medlb/article_detaillb.cfm?article_ID=ZZZ2K98T77C&sub_cat=2006.

9. "Facts in Brief: Induced Abortion," Alan Guttmacher Institute, Available at: www.guttmacher.org/pubs/fb_induced_abortion.html.

10. "Fact Sheet: Abortion in the U.S." The Henry J. Kaiser Family Foundation, January 2003.

11. "Is Abortion Safe? Physical Complications," National Right to Life. Available at: www.nrlc.org/abortion/ASMF/asmf13.html.

12. (Doe, 410 U.S. at 192)

13. "Roe Reality Check #2," United States Council of Catholic Bishops. Available at: http://www.usccb.org/prolife/RoeRealityCheck2.pdf.

Chapter 11:
Work in the Real World

1. "Women in the Labor Force: A Databook," Report 973, U.S. Department of Labor, Bureau of Labor Statistics, February 2004, 9.

2. Ibid., 6.

3. Ibid., 19.

4. National Institute of Child Health and Human Development Early Child Care Research Network, "Does Amount of Time Spent in Child Care Predict Socioemotional Adjustment During the Transition to Kindergarten," *Child Development*, July/August, 2003, Volume 74, Number 4, 976.

5. "20 Leading Occupations of Employed Women Full-time Wage and Salary Workers, 2003 Annual Averages," U.S. Department of Labor, Women's Bureau, April 25, 2005. Fact sheet available at: http://www.dol.gov/wb/factsheets/20lead2003.htm.

6. Charmaine Yoest, "What Do Parents Want?" *The American Enterprise*, May/June 1998.

7. "Motherhood Today—A Tough Job, Less Ably Done: As American Women See It," Pew Research Center for the People & the Press, May 9, 1997.

Chapter 12:
The Myth of Having It All

1. Betty Holcomb, *Not Guilty! : The Good News For Working Mothers* (Touchstone, New York, 2000) 35.

2. Ibid., 120.

3. "Motherhood Today—A Tough Job, Less Ably Done: As American Women See It," 7.

4. "Time-Use Survey," Bureau of Labor Statistics, Department of Labor, September 14, 2004. Available at: http://www.bls.gov/news.release/pdf/atus.pdf.

5. Warren Farrell, *Why Men Earn More* (American Management Association, New York, 2005).

6. Ibid., 27, 44.

7. Ibid., xxiv–xxv.

Chapter 13:
Daycare Delusions

1. "Child care in the United States is, by virtue of the character of the family, largely a system of private care. The parent-child unit is allegedly self-sufficient and, given the gender division of labor, the responsibility for

child care falls heavily on individual women. The experience of mothers (or other caregivers) is based on the assumption that children are best cared for by their biological mother. Exceptions to this design do exist, although even then the arrangements for child care are usually managed by the mother, and it is other women who do the work. Although it is more and more impractical to do so, mothers usually have the major responsibility for the everyday care of their children." Anderson, 189.

2. "A number of contemporary social problems are located in families. Violence against women in the family—in the form of battering, marital rape, and incest—reflects the powerlessness of women in society.... Finally, changes in family organization have created greater societal needs for child care. Resistance to organized child care stems, in part, from the continuing belief that only biological mothers can best care for children. In sum, new policies are needed that provide supports for the diverse needs of families and recognize the new demands placed by changing systems of work and family life." Ibid., 192-93.

3. Sapiro, 295.

4. Ibid., 435.

5. Hillary Rodham Clinton, *It Takes A Village* (Simon & Schuster, New York, 1996) 221–222.

6. "Conservatives further argue that the incentive for individuals to provide for their own families was stripped away by tax-supported public programs, especially those supporting the poor. Government intrudes in the family by telling parents how to care for and discipline children and how husband and wives should treat each other (e.g., by forbidding parents and husbands to beat their children and their wives)." Virginia Sapiro, 437.

7. Robertson, 135.

8. Melinda Gish, "Child Care Issues in the 107th Congress," Congressional Research Service, March 10, 2003, 5.

9. Lynne M. Casper, "Whose Minding Our Preschoolers?" Current Population Reports, Household Economic Studies, P70-53, U.S. Department of Commerce, Economics and Statistics Administration, March 1996, 1.

10. "Motherhood Today—A Tough Job, Less Ably Done: As American Women See It," 1.

11. Holcomb, 22.

12. Joan K. Peters, *When Mothers Work: Loving Our Children Without Sacrificing Ourselves* (Perseus Publishing, Cambridge, Massachusetts, 1997) 2.

13. Holcomb, 23.

14. Robertson, 42-43.

15. "Why have the NICHD study investigators never made it clear that the large majority of children experiencing poor-quality care function "in the normal range"? Why, in fact, when the study found, as it did two years ago, that low-quality care was related to more problem behavior when children were two and three years of age, was there no talk of aggression "in the normal range"? And why is it when higher levels of aggression and disobedience are found to be related to experiences like growing up in poverty or being reared by a depressed mother, that no one ever talks about aggression "in the normal range" as they so cavalierly do now when the issue is the depth of childcare experience?" Robertson, 54-55.

16. Ibid., 55.

17. Ibid., 71-72.

18. Ibid., 104.

19. National Institute of Child Health and Human Development Early Child Care Research Network, "Does Amount of Time Spent in Child Care Predict Socioemotional Adjustment During the Transition to Kindergarten," *Child Development*, July/August, 2003, Volume 74, Number 4, 978.

20. Ibid., 981.

21. Ibid., 989.

22. Eberstadt, xiv.

23. Ibid., 6.

24. Ibid., 8.

Chapter 14:
Politics: All Women Don't Think Alike

1. "Women in Elected Office: Fact Sheet Summaries," Center for American Women and Politics, Rutgers, The State University on New Jersey. http://www.cawp.rutgers.edu/Facts/Officeholders/cawpfs.html.

2. Ellen R. Malcolm, "Women Are A Huge Political Power—It's Time They Are Treated as Such," *Seattle Post-Intelligencer*, July 26, 2004.

3. Jane Musgrave, "Celebrities Rally Women Voters," Cox News Service, October 26, 2004.

4. Richard Matland and David King, 2002, forthcoming in Cindy Rosenthal, ed. *Women Transforming Congress.* (University of Oklahoma Press), 17. Available at: http://ksghome.harvard.edu/~dking/rosenthalchapter.pdf.

5. Tom W. Smith & Lance A. Selfa, "When Do Women Vote for Women," The Roper Center for Public Opinion Research, September/October, 1992.

6. Matland and King, 20.

7. Ibid., 16.

Chapter 15:
Divorcing Uncle Sam

1. Ruth, xii.

2. Ibid.

3. Ibid., xiii.

4. Ibid., 2.

5. Ibid., 16.

6. Ibid., 8.

7. For a more expensive discussion of this issue, see Sommers, *Who Stole Feminism.*

8. Ruth, xiii.

9. "Police Release 911 Tapes Of Woman Who Killed Intruder," WESH News, Orlando, Florida, May 31, 2005. Available at: http://www.wesh.com/news/4552505/detail.html.

10. Cancer Advocacy Coalition, News Release, "Deadly Silence Meets Growing Cancer Crisis," January 16, 2003. Available at: http://www.cancer-advocacycoalition.com/pages/2002-reportcard-news-release.htm.

11. Nadeem Esmail and Dr. Michael Walker, "Waiting Your Turn: Hospital Waiting Lists in Canada," 14th Edition, The Fraser Institute, October 2004, 31. Available at: http://www.fraserinstitute.ca/admin/books/chapterfiles/wyt2004%20pt2.pdf#.

12. Robertson, 126.

ACKNOWLEDGMENTS

I owe a deep debt of gratitude to the Independent Women's Forum—in particular, Michelle Bernard, Charlotte Hays, Heather Higgins, Ricky Silberman, Nancy Pfotenhauer, Christie Hobbs, Arianne Massey, and Jen Gustafson—for supporting me during the writing of this book. Thanks also to Lida Noory, Arrah Neilson, Bambi Little Juarez, Joy Downey, Tatiana Posada, and Alyson Gabel for their help with research.

I am grateful to the team at Regnery, Stephen Thompson, Harry Crocker, and Marji Ross, for giving me the opportunity to write this book.

Most of all, I am thankful for the support of my family and friends, including Julie Gunlock, April Ponnuru, Trish McDonough, Charlie Korsmo, Emily Porter, Frank Micciche, Retha and Ronald Lukas; my parents, Peter and Dianne Lips, who supported me in this and everything else; and, Brad and Cindy Lips for their thoughtful feedback.

A special thanks to my brother, Dan Lips, for his endless edits and counsel, and my husband, Aaron, the best editor and friend I could hope for.

This book is dedicated to my daughter, Molly Dianne.

INDEX

Index